Re-entry II

Re-entry II

John Wesley White

Foreword by Billy Graham

MOTT
MEDIA

RE-ENTRY II

ISBN 0-88062-044-7

Printed in Canada

CONTENTS

FOREWORD

The theme of *Re-Entry*, the second coming of Jesus Christ, is urgently needed in the preaching of the Church today. I am deeply concerned about war, poverty, pollution, racism, illiteracy, and crime, and I am doing everything I am able to do in order to get these ravaging scourges under control. But no one can read the facts and be unaware that things are getting worse instead of better—and they will continue to get worse and worse until Jesus Christ comes again to institute His program for peace and prosperity on this earth.

John Steinbeck told me before he died that he could see no hope for America unless we had a catastrophe. A catastrophe we may have, but I believe Jesus Christ is coming again and that He will save us from nuclear extermination. We have now reached the point where only He can. That is why the Church has a theology of hope. Winston Churchill asked me thirty years ago, "Young man, can you give me any hope?" I said to him, as I say to all, "Jesus Christ is our hope!"

The author of this book has been one of my associate evangelists since 1964, and he has been of invaluable personal assistance to me in the area of research. During his time with me, he has traveled to a hundred countries, preaching the Gospel from Minneapolis to Moscow, from Montreal to Melbourne. He is a compassionate and compellingly persuasive evangelist. In one of his crusades, held in Sioux Falls, South Dakota, over 2,000 inquirers came forward to make decisions for Christ. He has also had extensive TV ministry throughout North America. His weekly half-hour program with George Beverly Shea is now in its twelfth year.

John Wesley White is a native of Canada. There he played ice hockey and was vice-principal of a high school. Called into evangelism, he trained at the Moody Bible Institute and Wheaton College, both in Illinois. Moving to the British Isles, he did graduate research at Queens University and Trinity College in Ireland, and finally studied at Oxford University in

England from which he earned his doctorate. In addition to his evangelistic ministry, he has served for many years as chancellor of Richmond College in Toronto.

Re-Entry is a series of addresses which Dr. White initially gave in the world-famous Peoples Church in Toronto where he serves as an elder and where he regularly worships when he is home. These are not evangelistic sermons such as he would preach in a crusade, but are essentially a teaching rather than a preaching of the Gospel, and this, obviously, on only one doctrinal theme. Their uniqueness, and therefore their chief merit, lies in the fact that they focus almost entirely on the parallels between biblical signs which were specifically prophesied concerning the second advent of Jesus Christ and actual events which are currently transpiring all around us.

Probably no gospel theme apart from "Ye must be born again" is more relevant today, and I preach on some facet of this subject in virtually all of my crusades. Our world is filled with fear, hate, lust, greed, war, and utter despair. Surely the second coming of Christ, His "re-entry," is the only hope for replacing these depressing features with trust, love, universal peace and prosperity. For this the world, wittingly or inadvertently, waits.

Billy Graham
January, 1985

INTRODUCTION

As astronaut Marc Garneau soared into space aboard the *Challenger,* his wife Jackie was ecstatic. But she was even more exhilarated a fortnight later during his "re-entry."

It is an essential and integral part of the gospel to proclaim the resurrection and ascension of Jesus Christ. But only the "re-entry" of Jesus Christ can alleviate the escalating anxiety of a troubled and turbulent world. Jesus assuredly promised, "If I go away, I will come again." The "re-entry" of Jesus Christ will issue in triumphant life, glory, and eternal victory for the universal Church.

During the fortieth anniversary celebrations of D-Day, Al Mazerolle, a Canadian, returned for the first time to Normandy. He was greeted by Edith Bodin, who as a little girl had been ruthlessly shot by the retreating Nazis. The bullet lodged close to her heart, and she doubtless would have died had Al not *saved* her in a daring, selfless rescue, which took him to within an eyelash of death. With tears streaming down her cheeks, Edith threw her arms around Mr. Mazerolle and exclaimed, "Savior!" That one word said it all.

In similar fashion, St. Paul wrote of that climactic moment when the saints of all ages will experience "the glorious appearing of the great God and our Saviour Jesus Christ!" (Titus 2:13).

In the following chapters our theme will be "re-entry" —that is, the return of "our Saviour Jesus Christ." I have elected to quote profusely from the Scriptures on the one hand and current events on the other. I felt that rather than presenting my own views, I would prefer to point to what I consider astonishing parallels between contemporary news reports and biblical prophecies. Readers must be the arbiter by weighing the facts and drawing their own conclusions.

John Wesley White
Toronto, Canada
March, 1985

Chapter One

Theology and the Coming Christ

On September 14, 1984, millions around the world via TV and the 300,000 people gathered in Downsview, Toronto, heard Pope John Paul II exclaim, "Lord we're looking forward to your coming in glory." Having traversed the length and breadth of our country, the pope concluded his pastoral visit in Ottawa with these words, "We wait in joyful hope for the coming of our Lord and Savior Jesus Christ."

In November 1984, Dr. Alexander Haraszti described how, when he was setting up Billy Graham's meetings across the Soviet Union, he asked Metropolitan Filaret, chairman of the External Affairs Department of the Moscow Patriarchate of the Russian Orthodox Church, "Do you believe in the Second Coming?" only to be eagerly interrupted by the Metropolitan, "Of course, I believe in the Second Coming—the Second Coming of Jesus Christ!"

One hundred million North Americans heard Marvin Kalb of NBC ask President Reagan, during his final debate with Walter Mondale, "Do you feel that we are heading for Armageddon?" Mr. Reagan replied, "Yes, though no one on earth knows whether it's a thousand years away, or will occur the day after tomorrow. But yes, the biblical prophecies of what would portend the coming of Armageddon are surely falling into place." *Time* (November 5, 1984), commenting, undertook to encapsulate what Mr. Reagan believes, based on "the biblical prophecies of the End Times" and "eleven public and private utterances by Reagan on the possible imminence of Armageddon." *Time* affirmed that mainstream "Christian churches teach that the end of history will be marked by Christ's return to earth to establish a perfect Kingdom," so that "Christ's second coming will precede an actual millennial Kingdom . . . . Reagan is among the millions [who] believe Christians will be swept or 'raptured' into heaven before the Great Tribulation. 'Signs of the Times' [leading up to that Great Tribulation, but already unfolding toward their terrible fulfillment after the evacuation of Christians] will be history's worst; famines, wars, earthquakes, [and the most certain sign] the return of the Jewish people to the Holy Land, which began when Israel was founded in 1948. [This was followed inevitably by] Israel's capture of Old Jerusalem in 1967 [eventually making] possible the rebuilding of the Temple on its original site. [Meanwhile true believers await—while working intensely hard for Christ—the moment of their being] 'raptured' into heaven before the Great Tribulation [during which] the Soviet Union, the evil northern Empire of Ezekiel 38-39 [joined by Libya, Ethiopia and Iran—Ezekiel 38:5] will swoop down upon Israel but be defeated. After Armageddon, God will inaugurate the millennium." The *Time* article concludes, "When Christ really does break into this scene, there will be a lot of surprised people." The *London Times* quotes the *Jerusalem Post* as indicating that the above outline of future events reflects the belief of "the most powerful Christian element in America." According to the Gallup Poll, four times as many North Americans as the number who voted for President Reagan and Prime Minister Mulroney combined, believed in the second coming of Jesus Christ.

The second coming is good news. Della Reese belts out on TV, "Don't Bring Me No Bad News." The best answer to that one is: Jesus Christ is coming again and that's good news. It's only too apparent that ours is as anguished an age as it is angry. It is both ironic and paradoxical that man should be ripping in half as he is being catapulted upward, slingshot into space by a sophisticated scientism, while he is being savagely sucked from beneath by the woes of war, the stalking suffocation of pollution, proliferating poverty, raging racism and the ultimate weaponry which threatens thermonuclear annihilation. Schizophrenically split, he desperately yearns to become whole once again.

Mikhail Gorbachev, the head of the Soviet Union, omens,

"Never before has so terrible a threat loomed so large and dark over mankind as in these days." Here in Canada, our prime minister sees man "teetering on the brink of disaster, living with the ever-present threat that in the space of a few moments all our struggles, hopes, dreams and sacrifices could be reduced to contaminated rubble." In a Speech from the Throne, it is stated that the "nuclear threat preys upon the hopes and dreams of every man and woman on the planet!" Stephen Lewis, our ambassador to the United Nations, levels, "I simply believe, as all reasonable human beings believe, that if there is a nuclear war it will mean the end of the human race [as] simply and starkly as that." Our Ambassador for Disarmament, Douglas Roche, agrees, "Nuclear outbreak would lead to the extinction of man." *War*, the Sunday evening series of seven prime-time programs by the CBC-TV, concludes with Gwynne Dyer's summation in answer to a question by Patrick Watson on what the chances of nuclear war really are: "Man has perhaps a 5% [one in 20] chance of getting out of this century without being nuked. Nuclear war is like a landslide—you can see it coming, but you can't stop it."

A polling of North Americans under thirty reveals that a majority of them believe that an all-out nuclear war is likely within ten years. A front-page headliner reads *"Nuclear War Biggest Worry,"* detailing that seven times as many people are deeply worried about the prospects of impending nuclear war as are worried about inflation, six times as many worry about nuclear war as are concerned about who will win the next election, four times as many as are worried about the economy, and nearly three times as many as are worried about unemployment. Among those quoted were TV reporter Kevin Newman, who frankly expects a nuclear war in [his] lifetime. "I can't see any logical solution given the path of world events." Dr. George Ignatieff, a former ambassador to the United Nations, warns that, in addition to the possibility of a nuclear war being started deliberately or by miscalculation, it could be triggered "by accident." Currently, with some 63,000 nuclear bombs, there exists "a combined destructive power about one million times that of the bomb that leveled Hiroshima." That's enough to incinerate 100 billion people, 20 times the current population of the earth. Modern man experiences, in fact, a fulfillment of Jesus' pro-

phecy of "men's hearts failing them for fear, and for looking
after those things which are coming on the earth" (Luke 21:26).

As a consequence, far too many people increasingly turn to
the prophetic prognosis of astrology. It's the "in" thing for the
jet set. "Psychic Phenomena: Communication from Beyond?"
mesmerizes a national TV audience. In a craving to see forward,
people turn backward to an ancient Persian cult, astrology, and
diligently pore over its omens that appear in two out of every
three North American newspapers. Moderns will engage in star-
gazing or crystal-gazing. If they can't escape stark reality by going to the horses, there is the horoscope. Psychiatrists complain
that the clairvoyants and the Cassandras are doing them in.
UFOers and ESPers, Yoga masters, occultists, voodoo priests
and sorcerers, gurus and psychic seers with their spooky séances
are having a field day. The younger crowd of course prefer coke
and pot, for man is a chronic tripper. He must have a
psychedelic experience, even though hallucinogenic drugs may
induce him to jump insanely to his death.

The second coming of Jesus Christ is the only really satisfac-
tory answer to the lament of Dr. Ernest Howse, former
moderator of the United Church of Canada and perhaps our
most prominent liberal clergyman of the past generation. For
he, too, joins the Jeremiahs in opining that "the world is dark
with what seems like the sunset of civilization. Prophecies of
global disaster, which before would have been dismissed as
lunatic, are now seriously spoken, and everywhere stun the
minds with terrifying dreams and incomprehensible dread.
[People worldwide, facing down] an intolerable fate, are
rushing blindly to a crossroads encounter with doom."

Writing for the liberal Jewish community, Rabbi Reuben
Slonim notes, "Churches and synagogues have always insisted
that they carried a message of supreme importance for human
society. They promised to abolish war, establish the equity of all
men, prohibit the exploitation of human beings, and transform
the city of man into the city of God. Despite the collective efforts of all cults and creeds, the sword is still the sword, not a
plowshare." To that critique, surely there is one answer: the
coming of the Messiah! For millenia every devout Jew has
prayed daily, "I believe with complete faith in the coming of the
Messiah, even though He tarry, yet I will wait for Him every

coming day." Every premier and president Israel has had, has declared that the only ultimate hope for his country and for his people is the coming of the Messiah.

Man simply must have hope: future hope. Those theologians who don't believe in Christ's coming again capitulate to despair. Thomas J. J. Altizer, professor of Bible and Religion at Emory University, introduced his widely heralded "God is dead" theory in the sixties. Now he is obliged to write again, this time somberly, of the abject "hopelessness in today's world." That is why Bible prophecy in general and the second coming of Christ in particular are currently so relevant to the human situation.

Twelve hundred delegates from thirty-two countries gathered for the Jerusalem Conference on Bible Prophecy in what *Newsweek* labels "the first conference of its kind since A.D. 50." It was assembled under the co-chairmanship of a longtime editor of *Christianity Today*, who made it clear that the gathering had been convened to highlight current events as they related to the second coming of Jesus Christ. "We live already in the last days. . . . The last of those days is soon to break upon us."

Prophecy, that is, predictions of future events, occupies approximately one-quarter of all Scripture. The teaching of the second coming of our Lord is dealt with some 1,845 times in the Bible, 318 of these occasions being in the New Testament. The return of the Lord is the dominant theme of seventeen Old Testament books and one epistle in the New Testament. In fact, seven out of every ten chapters in the New Testament make reference to the second coming, and whole passages of the last half of the Bible are given over exclusively to its discussion. It is clear from the Scriptures that Christ is not only to be the subject but the object of our preaching. We are to proclaim not only the Christ of the second coming, but the second coming of Christ.

Overzealous soothsayers from time to time deliberately disobey Jesus Christ and predict dates for a forthcoming divine appearance, often bringing into disrepute one of the most precious and potent doctrines of the Christian Church. Archbishop Trench translated Mark 13:32, "If I were God, as well as man, even I should not know the day nor the hour." Jesus was emphatic that we should not set dates for this advent. A blatant example of the violation of Jesus' command occurred in Hertford, England. A local newspaper notice read, "The world is definitely coming to an end on Wednesday, December 11, at noon precisely. A full report will appear in this newspaper next Friday." When the Friday came, there was no doomsday to report, so the editor re-ran the article with his own postscript, "We're still here!"

However, these isolated instances of delusion must not be permitted to cause us to avoid the proclamation of Christ's return. God the Father, said Jesus, knows when He will send back His Son. In Toronto my three eldest sons were playing together on a forward line in a hockey game one night when there was a dispute between the referee and the timekeeper over when the game would end. "The game is over!" called out the one. "Two minutes to go!" asserted the other, adding, "My father is the Commissioner of this League and we're playing according to *his* time." The game went on for two more minutes! The world is running, not according to the timekeeping of scientists, statesmen, or well-meaning prognosticators, but according to the plan of God the Father.

Without hope, our world cannot go on. "What oxygen is to the lungs," observed Emil Brunner, "such is hope for the meaning of life." *Reader's Digest* affirms that to be happy we must have someone to love, something to do, and something to hope for. Christ provides all these for the believer, but only if we rest in His promise to come again. Hiley Ward of the *Detroit Free Press* calls for theology books on "hope." In fact, we have the one book of theology which offers hope—the Bible! But we need to read it and trust its message. "While we live this life," noted St. Paul, "we hope and wait for the glorious denouement of the great God and of Jesus Christ our Saviour."

The world hopes for the best, but Jesus Christ offers the best hope. An old year goes out with the newspaper headline, "A Year of Tragedy Saved by a Space Spectacular." Writers everywhere are speaking of a world in tragedy. Can it be saved? Yes, but only by a space spectacular: the return of Jesus Christ. A director of the National Aeronautics and Space Administration remarks, "Man has started his drive out into the universe, the beginning of a movement that will never stop." He is right. Someday Jesus Christ will come and free us forever from all gravitational drag: moral and mortal. When the Russians were about to launch one of their most sensational space shots, they announced that the venture would be a "final rehearsal for a cosmic journey." Mankind is in a final rehearsal for a cosmic journey, surrounded as he is by events which, according to scriptural forecasts, are harbingers of an eternal cosmic journey for the true Church of all ages. This turning toward *Space: A New Direction For Mankind* (as a book title expresses it) can add a whole new dimension to living.

Father Clifford Stevens, a Roman Catholic clergyman, proposes a new look at theology in the light of the aerospace age. He points out that, according to Einstein's theory, men who travel at or near the speed of light will experience a deceleration of time, so that a man in an ultrafast spaceship will age only a few months while his family and friends back on earth are living through decades and generations. Some scientists claim that when man can travel at the speed of electricity, "time will be no more," literally, for the aging process will cease. As well, the Russians announce that terrestrial fuel for space travel will soon be obsolete, for they have perfected a process of utilizing celestial nitrogen as fuel for space travel. This is evidence that the physics of eternity and infinity are breaking in upon us. St. John the Apostle wrote in his sunset years, "Beloved, now are we the sons of God, and it doth not yet appear what we shall be: but we know that, when he shall appear, we shall be like him; for we shall see him as he is" (1 John 3:2).

Just what basis do we have for entertaining such a euphoric prospect? This is not a new question. St. Peter foresaw that it would be asked! "In the last days there will come men who scoff at religion," anticipated St. Peter, "and they will say: 'Where now is the promise of his coming? Our fathers have been laid to their rest, but still everything continues exactly as it has always been since the world began'" (2 Peter 3:3,4 NEB). No Christian should permit himself to be denied for a moment the assurance that Jesus Christ is coming back. In fact, we are only really Christians if we believe that our Lord is returning. It was Jesus Himself who put forward that bedrock promise, "Set your troubled hearts at rest. Trust in God always; trust also in me. There are many dwelling-places in my Father's house; if it were not so I should have told you; for I am going there on purpose to prepare a place for you. And if I go and prepare a place for you, I shall come again and receive you to myself, so that where I am you may be also; and my way there is known to you" (John 14:1-4 NEB).

At this point, Thomas, the doubter, interrupts in a manner typical of anyone who is thoughtfully curious, "Lord, we do not know where you are going, so how can we know the way?" (John 14:5 NEB).

Jesus replies with the familiar words which obviously apply to His coming again, "I am the way; I am the truth and I am life: no one comes to the Father except by me" (John 14:6 NEB). To accept any of Jesus' words as authoritative means we must accept them all and none are more relevant than His promise, "I shall come again."

Plain as Jesus had made the promise of His coming again to His disciples, at the time of His ascension they still did not seem to grasp its significance. Five hundred disciples stood looking upward on that historic occasion as the Lord ascended. He detected their consternation and sent messengers of assurance: ". . . suddenly two men dressed in white stood beside them and said, 'Men of Galilee, why are you standing here looking up into the sky? This very Jesus who has been taken up from you into Heaven will come back in just the same way as you have seen him go' " (Acts 1:10,11, Phillips). As He went away, so He will come again. As He ascended, so He will descend to receive His Church into eternal glory.

When anyone reads or hears of this for the first time, it understandably sounds mysterious. "Listen!" St. Paul assured the Corinthians. "I will unfold a mystery: we shall not all die, but we shall all be changed in a flash, in the twinkling of an eye, at the last trumpet-call. For the trumpet will sound, and the dead will rise immortal, and we shall be changed. This perishable being must be clothed with the imperishable, and what is mortal must be clothed with immortality. And when our mortality has been clothed with immortality, then the saying of Scripture will come true, 'Death is swallowed up; victory is won!' 'O Death, where is your victory? O Death, where is your sting?' . . . God be praised, he gives us the victory through our Lord Jesus Christ" (1 Corinthians 15:51-57 NEB). It was this resplendent passage that was read at the funeral of Winston Churchill!

Nor was this teaching the private preserve of St. Paul. All of the apostles proclaimed this event as the zenith of history. The writer to the Hebrews exhorted Christians always to live as if in "a very little while, He that cometh shall come, and shall not tarry" (Hebrews 10:37, Phillips). St. James was concerned that believers should maintain a posture of vigilance, always, "patient and stout-hearted, for the coming of the Lord is near" (James 5:8 NEB). St. Peter explained that any number of trials can simply be treated as trails to triumph, since they will issue in "praise and honor and glory at the appearing of Jesus Christ" (1 Peter 1:7).

"Now, my children," wrote the aging St. John with tender love, "dwell in him, so that when he appears we may be confident and unashamed before him at his coming" (1 John 2:28 NEB). John seemed to feel that Jesus Christ would possibly come again during his lifetime. He probably based this on Jesus' words to Peter during the post-resurrection interlude, "If it is my wish for him [John] to stay until I come, is that your business, Peter?" (John 21:22, Phillips). The octogenarian John, as he concluded recording his Revelation of Jesus Christ on the Isle of Patmos, replied to our Lord's assertion, "Yes, I am coming very quickly!" by saying, "Amen, come, Lord Jesus!" (Revelation 22:20, Phillips).

Jude traced his doctrinal belief in the return of our Lord to antiquity, quoting how "Enoch also, the seventh from Adam, prophesied . . . saying, Behold, the Lord cometh with ten thousands of his saints, to execute judgment upon all, and to convince all that are ungodly among them of all their ungodly deeds which they have ungodly committed, and of all their hard speeches which ungodly sinners have spoken against him" (Jude 14, 15).

Alexander Maclaren aptly noted, "The primitive Church thought more about the second coming of Jesus Christ than about death or about heaven. They were not looking for a cleft in the ground called a grave, but for a cleavage in the sky called Glory. They were not watching for the 'undertaker,' but for the 'Uppertaker.' " In other words, they were not druggies looking for a cocaine high: they were believers looking for Christ from on high; they were not gamblers waiting at the Hialeah Course: they were Christians listening for the "Hallelujah Chorus"!

They felt that man's chief end was to get right with God, or to be left when Christ returned. Winston Churchill's favorite American song was "Mine Eyes Have Seen the Glory of the Coming of the Lord!" That was the vision of the ancient apostles: one which gave them dynamism and direction.

All the great catholic creeds of the Church give a climactic place to the return of Christ. To hear once or to repeat daily the Apostles' Creed is to know the impact of those resounding words, "From thence He shall come to judge the quick and the dead." The Nicene Creed affirms, "He shall come again with glory to judge both the quick and the dead" and the Presbyterian Confession of 1967 hails "the hope of His coming.

In addition, great figures in church history have witnessed to their own hope in Jesus' return. Augustine used to reason that when Jesus commanded, "Lazarus, come forth," He did so to limit the resurrection to the one man Lazarus. But in that great day, He would say, "Come forth," and the cemeteries of the world would yield up their Christian dead at His behest. "I live," exclaimed Martin Luther, "as though Jesus Christ died yesterday, rose again today and were coming again tomorrow." Every English-speaking Christian will forever be indebted to Tyndale for his Bible. He once described the motivation for his ministry as springing from the realization that "Christ and His apostles warned us to look for Christ's coming again every hour." As Bishop Ridley was being burned at the stake in front of Baliol College, Oxford, he exclaimed, "Let us with John, servant of God, cry, 'Come, Lord Jesus!' " Calvin, Bohler and Spangberg also referred often to the coming again of Jesus Christ. Two centuries later, when the Wesleys were rekindling the flame that the Reformers had spread, Charles Wesley made appeal to the return of Christ as the climactic goal for all Christian service. He thematically included it in 5,000 of his 7,000 hymns, reflecting the emphasis which his brother John gave to Christ's return in his preaching.

Jonathan Edwards was a watershed evangelist, theologian and philosopher of the mid-eighteenth century. His theology and his edition of the *Diary of David Brainerd* did so much to inspire the founding of the early missionary societies, and he also inspired new interest in the second advent of our Lord. Frontiersmen like William Carey, Henry Martyn and Alexander

Duff, zealous students of Edwards, were drawn to bring the Gospel to the ends of the earth largely because they believed that a precondition of Christ's return was, in the words of our Lord, that "this gospel of the kingdom shall be preached in all the world for a witness unto all nations; and then shall the end come."

The late Yale historian, Kenneth Scott Latourette, called the nineteenth century the "Great Century of Christian Missions." Eminent missionaries of the nineteenth century such as William Patton and David Livingstone, who heralded the Gospel in the dark and remote spots of the earth, and prominent churchmen in Europe and North America began to give a growing place to the scriptural teaching of our Lord's return. In England, Archbishop Trench held that the "second coming is possible any day; impossible no day." The voice to the masses, Charles Haddon Spurgeon, told his hearers that "the coming of the Lord is far more the hope of the Church than any remedial process, evolution or progresses among mankind."

Although her curiosity almost got the best of her on one or two occasions, Queen Victoria refused to break precedent with tradition and go to hear Spurgeon, a non-Anglican, expound. But both she and her chaplain, Dean Farrar, were as passionate believers in the second coming of Christ as was Spurgeon. During the service in Canterbury Cathedral on the first anniversary of the accession of Edward VII to the throne of England, Dean Farrar finally revealed how the late Queen, after hearing one of her chaplains preach at Windsor on the second coming of Christ, spoke to the dean about it and said, "Oh, how I wish that the Lord would come during my lifetime." "Why does your Majesty feel this very earnest desire?" asked Dean Farrar. With appropriate emotion, Queen Victoria replied, "Because I should so love to lay my crown at His feet."

At the coronation of Queen Elizabeth II in 1956, I happened to be in London. It was an unforgettable moment when the archbishop of Canterbury, Dr. Geoffrey Fisher, extended the crown to Her Majesty in the historic ceremony which states, "I give thee, O Sovereign Lady, this crown to wear, until He who reserves the right to wear it shall return."

In nineteenth-century America, the Episcopalian bishop Phillips Brooks was the voice of orthodoxy in proclaiming that "the coming of the Lord has been the inspiration of the Christian world. The power of any life lies in its expectancy." There were indeed innumerable crude and miscalculated distortions of this doctrine, especially on the American frontier, as over-zealous and unbalanced prophets announced dates, called out colonies of tarriers and made all sorts of weird predictions with regard to the second advent. To the sophisticated, these foreboding and disillusioning predictions of dates and places tended to bring the doctrine of the return of Christ into tragic disrepute. Nonetheless, the nineteenth century of Christian revival and world evangelism rode on the crest of a realization that there was a Mount Everest on the horizon, because Jesus Christ was coming again.

As the twentieth century began, many of the most able thinkers were no longer believers in the actual return of Christ. They resurrected the ideas of Plato, More, Fourier, Owen and Bellamy, insisting that man himself would eventually achieve utopia on this earth and that human nature was perfectible. W. E. Henley, who died in 1903, wrote, "I am the master of my fate; I am the captain of my soul." Optimism was in vogue. As a spokesman of modernist Christianity, Harry Emerson Fosdick articulated, "The kingdom is not something which comes down from heaven, but which is to be worked at among men."

But World War I came and the Englishman Sir Edward Grey lamented, "The lamps are going out all over Europe." It was a new era that had come crashing in on all the utopian dreams which had dominated the mind-managers of the previous generation. In fact, historians begin the twentieth century with 1914. According to secular humanists, war was to have been abolished, but, during the next 30 years, it wiped out as many lives as had perished in wars during the previous 800 years. In fact, the theories of man's nature being reformable had been exploded. By mid-century it was quite evident, as Dwight D. Eisenhower pointed out, that, unless there was a moral regeneration throughout the world, mankind could, on any given day, destroy itself with a nuclear explosion. But no prospect of a moral regeneration appeared. Man could not seem to bring himself to a state of repentance.

In 1860 the French scientist Pierre Bercelt had stated that "inside of one hundred years of physical and chemical science, man will know what the atom is. It is my belief that when science reaches this stage, God will come down to earth with His big ring of keys and will say to humanity, 'Gentlemen, it is Closing Time!' ''

One of Europe's most eminent churchmen, Pastor Niemoeller, had long looked upon the twentieth as "the Christian Century." But as the final quarter was being ushered in, he turned completely pessimistic regarding man's ability to survive. As Harold Lindsell points out in *Christianity Today*, man without God cannot survive. As ministers of the Word of God, "We are called upon to pronounce judgment on a society that is doomed; a society that cannot be saved until the coming of Jesus Christ." Thank God, Jesus is coming again.

For the last forty years, in the words of a U.S. president, the world has been a "powder keg that needs to be defused." Divisions are deepening, walls are heightening, and tensions sharpening. As the late French existentialist, Jean-Paul Sartre, lamented, "There is no escape from the present dilemma." "How shall we escape," asked the writer to the Hebrews, "if we neglect so great salvation?" (Hebrews 2:3). "Escape the damnation of hell, " exhorted Jesus Christ (Matthew 23:33). On being awarded the Einstein Peace Prize late in 1984, Pierre Elliott Trudeau quoted Blaise Pascal (France's greatest scientist ever, and—late in life—a fervent Christian), "If eternal damnation is possible, no sacrifice is too great to prevent that possibility from becoming reality." Pascal obviously refers to what every man, woman and child requires—personal salvation in Christ.

The hope of ultimate salvation, however, hinges on the coming again of Jesus Christ. Fifty million more North Americans believe in the afterlife today that did so forty years ago. *Psychology Today* polls its half-million readers and reveals that a majority actually "yearn" for eternal life, just as did the rich young ruler. There is a new looking to the celestial for the manifestation of the Son of God. *Time* devotes its religion section to "the theology of Hope," a revised phenomenon of German theologians. Conceptions of Christ's coming again vastly differ, but it is the one theme which defies neglect in an age dominated by pessimism.

The *New York Times* carries on its front page the forebodings of the late British author C.P. Snow, who believed our world is beleaguered with insoluble problems. Each year, he noted, the pessimism deepens. He left the impression that civilization was about to be abolished unless there was a divine intervention. Walter Lippmann put it, "For us all, the world is disorderly and dangerous, ungoverned and apparently ungovernable." Who will restore order? Who alone can govern this world? The answer is Jesus Christ. Thank God, He is coming again!

So it is with considerable interest that we listen to Father Joseph Christie on "The Sacred Heart Hour" speak from the prophecy of Joel on our Lord's return; that we read the statements of the mayor of Nazareth on the occasion of the pope's visit, regarding "the second coming of Christ"; that we read of Eugene Carson Blake, who writes, "I want you to know that I still believe as I was taught in my youth, that the second coming of Jesus Christ is an important and vital part of the full rounding of the Christian faith"; and that we read of the late Kenneth Scott Latourette, former president of the American Historical Society, who replied to a questioner, "I believe that our Lord may return at any time and bring this present stage of history to an end. That may well come between now and the year A.D. 2000."

The young, too, are aware of the Lord's return. Many follow the precedent of Bob Dylan, who was converted to Christ in the late seventies. Dylan, who is Jewish, made the second coming of Christ the theme of his album *Slow Train Comin'*. When he was touring Europe and the British Isles during the summer of 1984, Dylan drew vast crowds to his concerts where they heard him tell of Christ and how "He's comin' back to get us!"

Surely one of the most moving scenes, seen by millions of North Americans in the mid-eighties on network TV, was a religious documentary shot in a church in the Soviet Union, where beleaguered Christians were singing with an unworldly exuberance those thrilling lyrics learned by many of us in our childhood:

> When the trumpet of the Lord shall sound
> And time shall be no more,
> And the morning breaks eternal, bright and fair;

> When the saved of earth shall gather
> Over on the other shore,
> And the roll is called up yonder, I'll be there.

And who else but Paul Harvey could comment so poignantly that this golden oldie has indeed moved right back into the consciousness of Middle America!

Chapter Two

Science and Technology and the Coming Christ

Pierre Berton that most-read of Canadian writers in the 1980s, alleges in *The Comfortable Pew* that, in every battle between the Scriptures and science since Copernicus, the Bible has lost. Nothing could be so untrue! For one thing, it is because of science that mankind currently dangles over the precipice of doom. Winston Churchill perhaps put it best when he warned before his death: "The stone age may return on the gleaming wings of science and may even bring about its total destruction. Beware, I say, time is short."

It is the Bible, on the other hand, which reveals the salvation of Christ, the only viable option open to man. What Berton might have said is that religious zealots construct a superstructure of hypotheses on the alleged foundation of the Scriptures; that students of science construct what W. R. S. Thompson, director of the Commonwealth Institute of Biological Control in Ottawa, in his introduction to Charles Darwin's *Origin of the Species* (New York, 1959) calls "those fragile towers of hypotheses based on hypotheses, where fact and fiction intermingle in an inextricable confusion." It is when the highly biased defenders of these two fabricated bastions clash that the sophistries of the latter seem often to prevail intellectually over the frequent ingenuousness of the former. Thankfully, this posture is finally turning around. Dr. Roger Oakland, a former professor of biology at the University of Saskatchewan, testifies that he was a lifetime proponent of Darwinian evolution until he finally realized the hypocrisy of its hypotheses. Its premises simply could not be supported by fact. Therefore he began to explore creation as taught in the Bible, and he found every scriptural statement pertaining to man's origins consonant with the facts of science. It is refreshing to read in *Time* that "reputable scholars now believe" that the Bible after all is "reliable history." And as its history is reliable, so are its prophecies.

It seems to me that the billions of years in the past and of the future are bound closely together in the physics of God's master plan. St. Peter prophesied that "the day of the Lord will come as a thief in the night; in which the heavens shall pass away with a great noise" (2 Peter 3:10). It is currently accepted by some of the world's foremost astrophysicists that some 18 billion years ago the universe came into existence suddenly—many say candidly that the first cause was a creative act of God. This is well known as the big bang theory. As cited in *Time* magazine, a distinguished team of astronomers, taking their data from a radio telescope one mile long, announced that they suspect that they may be hearing across millions of light-years reverberations of the "Big Bang with which all creation came into existence billions of years ago." This sheds light on the integrity of the Genesis opening, "In the beginning God created the heavens and the earth."

And as creation came into existence, so it will go out—with a "Big Bang." (Does this not sound amazingly similar to the phrase "a great noise"?) This is the prevalent theory among astrophysicists today. *Time* also quotes two eminent geophysicists as stating that "if the magnetic field of the earth continues to run down at its present rate, the earth has less than 2,000 years until Doomsday." In yet another issue of *Time*, an M.I.T. professor reasons that it is entirely possible that an asteroid could well collide with the earth at any time and turn it back into a blob of molten lava. Speaking to Walter Cronkite on CBS, Ray Bradbury states that the sun is due eventually to blow up, or be blown up, in a huge celestial explosion. *The Day the Earth Caught Fire* and *2001: A Space Odyssey* show the cinema-goer the terrible and magnificent aspects of future activity in space. "The stars shall fall from heaven," Jesus prophesied in connection with His coming again and the end of the world (Matthew 24:29). The *Indianapolis Star* displays a photograph taken by the Palomar Observatory in California with an account of an explosion in the heart of a galaxy of stars which is currently cutting a swath sixty billion miles wide and rolling forward at the rate of twenty million miles an hour. Clearly, the universe is by no means as static as once thought.

As illustration of how the scientific world has turned from a supposed universal vogue of non-faith to one of much more belief, one could cite many of the astronauts, practicing precisionists, whose lives depend on accurate scientific data. Most charismatic of the astronauts is Colonel Frank Borman, currently president of Eastern Airlines and probably the most popular American ever to visit the Soviet Union. It was this outspoken Christian who introduced from the moon orbit the creation account from Genesis 1. Frank Borman believes in science and technology in their most advanced form; and yet, like the majority of his fellow astronauts (as he puts it), he believes in the Bible, adding, "The more we learn about the wonders of our universe, the more clearly we are going to perceive the Hand of God."

This point was also made by Prince Philip while on a recent visit to Toronto. With poignant solemnity he cautioned that, unless "the high priests of science" were prepared to subordinate their discoveries to an orientation which would be dominated by faith in God, there would cease to exist a basis of belief for man's survival on this planet. This is a sobering observation: if scientists ignore God, man will lose his life. "In many ways," laments Oregon senator Mark Hatfield, "God has been replaced by technology and we worship at the altar of materialism. When we are in trouble, we rely on the Technological Fix instead of Faith."

Byron Bangert in *Time* (December 3, 1984) pleads for the case that science and faith become "not enemies but essential complements, however much in tension they may exist." Pascal is invoked, "If we submit everything to reason, our religion will have nothing in it mysterious or supernatural. If we violate the principles of reason, our religion will be absurd and ridiculous."

God's books of science and Scripture never contradict each other. I have never seen a shred of evidence to support the comparably fallacious conjectures that the findings of science are sinister or that it is no longer viable to hold to the fidelity of the Scriptures. One of history's prominent scientists, Francis Bacon, put forward his own views on this in his *Advancement of Learning*, "Let no man, out of a weak conceit of sobriety, or an ill-applied moderation, think or maintain, that a man can search too far or be too well studied in the book of God's Word, or in the book of God's works . . . but rather let men endeavor an endless progress or proficiency in both."

During the Middle Ages, Western man, it seems, was prepared to believe anything religion did or said. For the last hundred and fifty years, by contrast, there have been those who have been prepared to believe anything a student of science says, actual or apocryphal. But today, as we quest for truth, we like to look harder. Science may be revealing much that once could be thought of only as fiction, but as former chancellor Solandt of the University of Toronto points out, science does not solve the basic problems of living. "The nineteenth century witnessed the loss of faith in God and the kingdom of heaven," reasoned the late Eric Hoffer, adding that "we are witnessing the loss of faith in man and the kingdom of heaven on earth."

All of this leads us to say that man needs a new order. Science can facilitate, but not fulfill. God alone can provide for our fulfillment, and He has an agenda for our future and His program is to send back His Son to set up His kingdom of peace and prosperity. Meanwhile, a look at contemporary science and technology confirms conditions which the Scriptures state would prevail at the time of Christ's coming again.

In the fourth verse of his last chapter, the prophet Daniel predicted that at "the time of the end . . . knowledge shall be increased." The Hebrew translation of these words could be much stronger, i.e., "A sudden knowledge explosion will occur at the time of the end." On this basis we must surely be at least in the fringe zone of "the time of the end." Currently, knowledge is doubling every ten years, and printed materials are doubling every fifteen years. "We're living in an information age, and information is limitless," observes social scientist Norman Feingold. Forty percent of all North Americans between eighteen and twenty-one years of age are in university or college today, double the number of forty years ago. Eighty percent of all the scientists in history are alive today. There are 20,000 different scientific journals being published regularly, many with a worldwide circulation. Seventy percent of the medicines used today have been developed since World War II.

But it is the computer, a mere three decades old, which is defining our times as the age of information. Because of computers something as ordinary as a credit card can carry 420 items of information on it. Computers enable children to play video games, cooks to program microwave ovens, airlines to book space for travel, sports teams to have a book on every athlete on the continent, governments to have incredible details on all their citizens, and police forces to have records of all lawbreakers. One computer can perform 55 billion transactions in one second. For example, when Apollo XIII ran into trouble 205,000 miles from earth, scientists working with computers figured out the correct return flight path for the crippled craft in just eighty-four minutes. Working with pencil and paper in the precomputer age, it would have taken a concentrating scientist 1,040,256 years. Today, man is even preparing to fight wars in space by computer.

The computer is changing our lifestyles in other ways also. The computer has in the past and will continue to greatly affect employment. In its tremendous efficiency in tasks such as billing, accounting, and word-processing, it replaces the work of many. Also, as robots become more and more sophisticated, more jobs are lost. Already robots sort letters and do assembly line work in manufacturing plants. Bob Hepburn reckons that robots have already taken over 700,000 Canadian and seven million American jobs, and, by the end of the century, the number of robots will treble. Their proliferation and sophistication in Japan, where they have reached their highest development, are the primary reason for that country's incredible success in the car market.

The computer is changing our lifestyles in other ways also. The *Chicago Tribune* peers into the future to predict Americans living in modular plastic homes, ordering their meals from a computer, spraying on their clothing and working only for enjoyment. Television sets today have converters to tape programs for later viewing; and converters may also be connected into a central computer bank, so that programs on any theme the viewer may wish to watch can be selected at will. Whole homecooked meals can be programmed ahead of time, their preparation and cooking being automated by computer. People step out of their homes into cars filled with computer-operated gadgets, telling them verbally to close the door, fasten their seat belts, slow down, get a fuel fill-up or watch out—the policeman is following. As people travel, wristwatch TV sets will soon be as common as transistor radios were in the seventies.

Many people ask whether or not there is an intimation of television in the Bible. For centuries and perhaps especially since such books as Professor Urey's (the winner of the Nobel Prize) *The Red Lights of the Apocalypse* appeared, fascination has centered on Revelation 11. We read that "when they [the two witnesses] have completed their testimony . . . their corpses will lie in the street of the great city where also [their] Lord was crucified. For three days and a half men from . . . every language and nation, gaze upon them." Indeed, "All men on earth gloat over them" (7-9, NEB). This statement seemed bizarre and ludicrous until such a scenario was made possible by television with the help of space satellites such as the pioneer Telstar and Early Bird. An estimated one billion people, at one time, watched transfixed as Neil Armstrong set foot on the moon. A similar number viewed the funeral of Konstantin Chernenko in 1985.

Certainly, TV would be an ideal device for the Antichrist to employ in order to impose his iron grip on the world, as Billy Graham pointed out on national TV (December 8, 1984). On the other hand, TV is the vehicle by which Billy Graham himself is able to preach the gospel to much of the world, including, in 1984, the Soviet Union. On "The 700 Club," Pat Robertson and I discussed Revelation 14:6, "And I saw another angel fly in the midst of heaven, having the everlasting gospel to preach unto them that dwell on the earth, and to every nation, and kindred, and tongue, and people." Might that flying "angel" (communication agent, as angel means) be the satellite in the sky which transmits the preached Gospel throughout the world? Also, TV is a way to make it possible for all people living at the time of Christ's advent to earth to "see the Son of Man coming in a cloud with great power and splendor!" (Luke 21:27, Phillips). "Behold he cometh," noted John in Revelation 1:7, "and every eye shall see him."

Stockpiles of information are not, in themselves, either good or bad. What matters is the use to which such knowledge is put. "A wise man will hear, and will increase learning," exhorted Solomon in his first chapter of Proverbs, predicating this on the realization that "the fear of the Lord is the beginning of knowledge" (Proverbs 1:7). However, it is well-known today, that, to many moderns, God is neither the beginning nor the end of knowledge. He is simply ignored, if indeed His existence is admitted at all. As Paul wrote to the Romans, "Thus, because they have not seen fit to acknowledge God, he has given them up to their own depraved reason" (Romans 1:28 NEB).

Why is it that, just when humanity is reaching the heights of knowledge, it is imperative that Jesus Christ come again? Because, as Paul wrote to the Corinthians, " 'Knowledge' breeds conceit" (1 Corinthians 8:1 NEB). Also, in the words of the ancient Jeremiah, "Every man is brutish in his knowledge" (Jeremiah 10:14). We are only just now beginning to realize this. A team of scholars was commissioned by the United States government to prove that education lessens crime. To their complete surprise and disillusionment, the team announced three years and several hundred thousand dollars later that, as an outcome of their research, they had discovered that education, in fact, escalates crime. Computer crime, which costs society billions of dollars annually, is a graphic example of this. Man's need for the return of Christ increases in direct proportion to his increase in knowledge.

Another condition that Daniel foresaw would prevail at the "time of the end" was that "many shall run to and fro." The prophet was referring to the whole realm of human transportation in which travel would carry men in prodigious vehicles from one point to another at incredible speeds and in ever-shortening times. In Isaiah 31:5 we read the prophecy that "as birds flying," so would be the defense of Jerusalem. Who could read this and not relate it to the events of today or to the much more astonishing prospects of tomorrow? A century and a half ago, who could have imagined a world in which the steam engine, the internal combustion engine, the electric motor, the jet engine, and now the thermonuclear-fueled motor would propel man across land and sea, up through the air and, far beyond, into space? The supersonic Franco-British Concorde on its transatlantic flights or, for that matter, the TU144 with Aeroflot, transports 130 passengers 4,000 miles at 1,500 miles per hour: twice the speed of sound. Astronauts have traveled 233,000 miles away from home and have cruised along at 24,630 miles per hour. Boeing's jumbo jets routinely carry up to 500 passengers at once. When one is able, as I was, to hold an early morning service in Sydney, Australia, and that same night preach the evening service in a church in Johannesburg, some 8,000 miles away, one realizes how far we've come since the Wright brothers first test-flew an aircraft in 1904. Travel is getting to be a way of life.

Throughout the Scriptures, we are repeatedly told that the coming of Christ will be accompanied by the sound of a trumpet. A physics laboratory in upper New York state has demonstrated that a large steel ball can be hoisted and held aloft in midair by focusing an intense beam of high-frequency sound waves under the ball. The ultrasonic sound was of too high a frequency to be detected by the human ear. This phenomenon is the kind of thing that could happen when Christ returns to rapture (Latin, "to snatch away") His Church into the celestial. "The Lord Himself shall descend from heaven with a shout"; . . . Christians of all ages "shall be caught up together to meet the Lord in the air." Those whose faith is in Christ, who are alive or deceased, will respond to the trumpet call. To those without faith, the only realization will be that true believers in Christ are suddenly gone.

Paul promised to those who ascend that the moment the Savior, our Lord Jesus Christ, catches us up, He'll "change our vile [temporal] body that it may be fashioned like unto his glorious body, according to the working whereby he is able even to subdue all things unto himself" (Philippians 3:21). In 1983 the Russians placed *Salut 7* in orbit as the first "permanent Soviet space station," but, as *Time* points out, when the cosmonauts go up there for six months or more they suffer from "atrophied muscles, weakened bones, a shrinking heart (by 10%) and space sickness renamed by NASA 'space adaptation syndrome.' " For the believer in Christ, however, there will be no space sickness, for there will be an immortal glorified body replacing these mortal ones.

Is man's flight into space to be found in scriptural prophecy? This is a frequently asked question. Assuming that several of the astronauts who went into space were Christians, whatever would happen if the second coming of Christ were to occur while they were aloft in space? Jesus Christ foretold that "with a trumpet blast he will send out his angels, and they will gather his chosen from the four winds, from the farthest bounds of heaven on every side" (Matthew 24:31 NEB). The majority of Bible scholars with whom I am acquainted think that this reference relates to the "revelation" of Jesus Christ and will occur seven years after the rapture. Hence, there would be time for large numbers of His "chosen" to be out in space somewhere. It seems to me it could also happen in measure at the time of the rapture. Angels therefore will fulfill the behest of our Lord to gather the saints together wherever they are. And we will, as Jeremiah prophesied, "mount up to heaven."

Ray Bradbury, author of *Martian Chronicles*, in conversation with Walter Cronkite on CBS-TV reckons that interplanetary travel will drive men back to God and the church because of the sharpened loneliness it will impose upon them. It also seems to me that if man cannot cope with lostness on this earth, what will he do when he begins to traverse the heavens? The Christian hope is that Christ will come again and liberate believers forever from terrestrial limitations.

Several other biblical incidents are rendered credible, even comprehensible, by man's venture into space. It used to be asked, How could Jesus walk on water? Is it not relevant today to reason that if a son of man—Russian or American—can walk in space, the Son of God could walk on the Sea of Galilee? Or that if the *Discovery* astronauts could walk out of their spaceship in 1984 and rescue satellites, "lost in space," that Jesus Christ as God the Son could come to earth from outer space to seek and to save the lost of this confusing planet?

From cover to cover the Bible refers to the fact that the coming of the Lord is immediately to be followed by a judgment. Secularists used to smile when it was stated that "God shall judge the secrets of men by Jesus Christ"; or, as Jesus Himself put it, "By a man's word shall he be justified and by a man's words shall he be condemned." But informed people are reluctant to smile anymore, for through sophisticated instrumentation, it is now possible to extract from solids, conversations which were made nearby them at a given time in the past. For example, it may presently be possible to recover from a nearby stone the actual voice of Moses as he replied to God at the burning bush. The vibrations are still there, somewhere—they need only be located, isolated, extracted and recorded. Every sound leaves a sound track. Telepathists are now convinced that every thought leaves its vibration trail somewhere. If men can do this, what can God do? Think of it! God summons the judgment and someone protests that he never said, did or thought a certain thing which shows up on his record. So Gabriel, say, goes from the court and brings in "Exhibit 'E' " and a stone cries out the truth.

A news item throws light on this matter of the judgment. The Soviets are now surveying the United States three out of every four days from a satellite network which is so thorough that it can photograph the seams of baseballs being pitched in Yankee Stadium and can reveal the numbers of shingles on houses in every part of the United States. And U.S. intelligence of the Soviet Union is comparably detailed, not only via video, but also via audio detection devices. For example, when the Korean airliner 007 was shot down by the Soviets in 1983, the Americans—and Japanese—were able to reveal every single coded message exchanged by the Soviet military: which makes sense out of a statement like "All things are naked and opened unto the eyes of Him with whom we have to do."

The invention of the first atomic bomb began right here in Canada—in Ontario—at Chalk River, remonstrated Dr. Helen Caldicott of Harvard in a CBC address on December 5, 1984. (She doesn't believe in the fear of God, because she doesn't believe in a personal God. Therefore, there was little hope in her oratory.) In the most frightening rhetoric that I have ever heard Caldicott described what would happen if a 20-megaton bomb were to be dropped on Toronto (such a bomb the Soviets currently have in place and ready on a missile warhead.) One-millionth of a second after detonation, the bomb would be burning a skyscraper-sized hole in the ground with a blowtorch heat that would soar to 150 million degrees Fahrenheit—approximately the temperature of the center of the sun. Toronto would not be just molten lava, much of it would be vaporized and ascend in a mammoth mushroom. Caldicott, giving the gory statistical estimates of what would happen in the widening concentric circles of devastation, reached an almost hysterical—if it weren't so terrifying—pitch with the announcement that, worldwide, the death toll would be one billion people from that one bomb alone. It was Helen Caldicott who was the focus of the Canadian National Film Board's 1983 Oscar-winning *If You Love This Planet*, a picture which not only horrified millions but also predicted that, unless a dramatic revolution installed peace throughout the world among all nations, man would annihilate himself in a nuclear war in the 1980s. It was indeed scary stuff.

But let's face it, such a scenario is very close to St. Peter's prophecy: "The day of the Lord will come as a thief in the night; in which . . . the elements shall melt with fervent heat; [and] the earth also and the works that are therein shall be burned up" (2 Peter 3:10). This is immediately comprehensible today to a scientifically oriented society. Up until half a century ago, it seemed to many to be ludicrous, if not quite comic: but not now. Not for those who have visited Hiroshima or Nagasaki, nor for those who are familiar with thermonuclear weapons. It has been suggested by Hebrew scholars that when Sodom and Gomorrah were being destroyed, God may have used an atomic explosion, for when Lot's wife, whom Jesus told us to remember, "looked back . . . she became a pillar of salt" (Genesis 19:26). The word for "salt" might be rendered "ash." There is a gory parallel in those who turned and looked back at the Nagasaki conflagration and were turned into ashen columns (something to which Helen Caldicott made reference in her address). Inexplicably, others who fled with their coats over their heads escaped untarnished. As the *Sydney Herald* put it, "Scientists have now discovered Doomsday fire!" A U.S. president warns that if another world war breaks out, it will be so devastating that all the previous wars of history, compared with it, would be like tossing a firecracker up against the surface of the sun.

St. Peter in that passage on "the Day of the Lord" (a passage in which he makes room for a series of destructive events by stating that "a day is with the Lord as a thousand years") clearly indicates that "the earth also and the works that are therein shall be burned up" (2 Peter 3:10). The annihilation of all life on this planet would now take a mere six minutes, and, in the current circumstances, would most likely be triggered by "an errant computer," warns peerless scientist Dr. David Suzuki (in an address to the Toronto Empire Club on December 6, 1984). A president of France thinks it more likely that a very "evil" man or regime will do it, because modern man has in him the seeds of his own self-destruction. Eminent professor and scientist Dr. Linus Pauling, who appeared on the same network TV program as I did in November 1984, reckons that there are now enough thermonuclear explosives stockpiled to equal 20 one-ton bombs for every acre on earth.

I descended into an American Minuteman missile silo some time ago and saw how one of thousands of these readied ICBMs could be triggered off and within a matter of minutes turn a city halfway around the world into what the commanding general described as an apocalyptic lake of fire and brimstone. Terrifying enough reading was provided a few years ago by Herman Kahn's *On Thermonuclear War*. David Inglis, the senior physicist at the Argonne National Laboratory in Washington, warns in his *Unless Peace Comes* of a hydrogen bomb wrapped in cobalt which can annihilate all life in the northern hemisphere, where three billion people live. Jonathan Schell and Freeman Dyson write in *The New Yorker*, as quoted by *Time* (June 11, 1984), that there exists a nuclear warhead today that, if detonated, "could touch off a chain reaction leading to the extinction of the human race." For three decades now, Nobel Prize-winner Harold Urey has feared a thermonuclear chain reaction which could not be stopped.

Is it any wonder that Jesus solemnly cautioned of a time of great tribulation "such as has never happened from the beginning of the world until now, and will never happen again?" (Matthew 24:21, Phillips). So terrible will be the maelstrom of woe that Jesus declared, "If that time of troubles were not cut short, no living thing could survive" (Matthew 24:22 NEB). Bible scholars have calculated from scriptural prophecy that approximately half of the human race will be wiped out by apocalyptic wars and woes. But, thank God, just when man is about to annihilate himself and everything living is about to be demolished, "for the sake of God's people those days are to be shortened" (Matthew 24:22, Phillips). "As lightning flashes across from east to west so will the Son of Man's coming be" (Matthew 24:27, Phillips). What person with a heart could ever have misgivings over the second advent of our Lord? For, were He not to come, man would annihilate himself.

"Every man, woman, and child lives under a nuclear Sword of Damocles," warned John F. Kennedy, "hanging by the slenderest of threads, capable of being cut at any moment by accident, or miscalculation, or by madness." That slenderest of threads will be severed by "man's inhumanity to man." But God be thanked, that all-exterminating thermonuclear Sword of Damocles will be caught in midair by the returning Savior.

Science and technology are largely where they are today because of frenzied efforts by the nations to research, invent, and mass-produce weapons which are capable of vanquishing their adversaries; "all sorts of armour" is how biblical prophecy describes it. In answer to His disciples' question, "What will be the signal for your coming and the end of this world?" Jesus said, "You will hear of wars and rumors of wars" (Matthew 24:3,6, Phillips). During the pre-world war period, classical Christianity came perilously close to ignoring this ominous portent. The hard facts since have driven men to face grim reality. John F. Kennedy called the world in general and America in particular to "a long twilight struggle, year in and year out . . . a struggle against . . . war itself."

The cost of weaponry worldwide is truly astronomical! Vice-President E. L. Velikkov of the Soviet Academy of Sciences wonders, "With more and more money, with more and more scientists, more and more work" being put into researching and manufacturing doomsday weaponry, does "peace" really have a chance? The same day, the U.S. Arms Control and Disarmaments Agency calculated that, in 1983, 800 million dollars were spent worldwide for weapons and other military purposes (up 323% in a decade), and in 1984 it rose to a trillion. That is sixty percent more than is spent on education and more than three times the amount invested in public health. Put bluntly, man is three times as desirous to kill as he is to render healing to his fellowman. We talk of universal brotherhood, but there seems to be more "hoods" than "brothers" emerging. According to Senator Mark Hatfield, there is currently the equivalent of twenty tons of TNT for each of the five billion humans on earth.

In Caesar's day, when our Lord prophesied "wars and rumors of wars" prior to His return, it cost seventy-five cents for the Roman army to kill an enemy soldier. By the First World War this cost had risen to $15,000; during the Second World War to $30,000; during the Korean War, to $50,000; in Vietnam it cost the Americans just over a million dollars for every Viet Cong they killed. Is it any wonder that the world was captivated by Barry Maguire's rendering of the "Eve of Destruction," or by Meryle High with "This world is headed for destruction, like Ancient Rome; this world is doomed; Jesus, take a hold and lead us through"?

I have been in Red Square, Moscow; I have traveled from the bottom to the top of South Vietnam; I have seen northern India and central Africa. And everywhere the most impressive machines were the military weapons: "all sorts of armour," a phrase the ancient prophet used to describe how the Russians would be equipped (Ezekiel 38:4). In Reagan's second administration, there is a lot more talk of peace between the USSR and the United States. However, with the Soviets installing a hundred more SS-20s in 1984, the Americans adding one hundred more Cruise and Pershing II missiles, and both sides escalating the arms buildup, in spite of negotiations, could that be called progress?

Dr. George Kistiakowsky, known as "the father of the nuclear trigger" for the crucial role he played in the Manhattan Project of the 1940s, does not hesitate to warn, "Nuclear war is becoming inevitable . . . and the threat is real and . . . the devastation will be unbelievable." To the apathetic he cautions, "Don't kid yourself, you will be one of the victims . . . nuclear weapons will be used somewhere between now and the end of the century." Adds Kistiakowsky's current colleague and former collaborator on the Manhattan Project, Jerrod R. Zacharias: the use of nuclear weapons will spell "extinction" of the human species from this planet. Sums up the third member of the Harvard/M.I.T./Manhattan Project troika Victor F. Weisskopf (who currently serves as advisor to the Vatican on nuclear issues because he fears that the nuclear threat is something only God can be trusted with anymore): "With the discovery of fission, mankind entrained cosmic forces with human irrationality." Only "a miracle" from God can save man from nuclear "holocaust."

"Miracle" deliverance of man by God is increasingly acknowledged in media releases today. When a professor of cardiology at Harvard, Dr. Bernard Lown, was addressing 15,000 Rotarians at Rotary International in Maple Leaf Gardens, Toronto, he pleaded, "Stop this race to Armageddon!" "We're doomed," he sighed. "[It] would be short of miraculous if we can end this century . . . without a nuclear" war. Broods Volkmar Deihe, "There is an increasing feeling that, like drug addicts, the leaders of nations today are hooked on nuclear death weaponry."

An estimated 63,000 nuclear bombs are currently allocated throughout the continents and oceans of the world, and, according to *Time*, ten new ones are being made every day. President Reagan has announced that the U.S. is in the process of adding 17,000 new nuclear bombs to its already formidable force. Until the advent of Star Wars (Strategic Defense Initiative) in the mid-1980s, the American defense system against nuclear attack from the Soviets had been based on TRIAD (land, air and sea forces) which means, first of all, the worldwide deployment of a network of land-based ballistic missiles which are classified as short-range, medium, and intercontinental. There are, secondly, the bombers deployed to U.S. strategic bases throughout the world and poised to carry nuclear warheads into any potential enemy target area. And, thirdly, there are nuclear submarines which circle the oceans and seas of the world with rocket power poised to unleash nuclear holocaust upon any country. While it is conceded that the Soviets have a big lead in nuclear submarine strength (*Jane's Fighting Ships*), American submarines can rain 9,632 nuclear bombs on Soviet soil. As Greer Boyce points out, "One U.S. Poseidon submarine carries 16 missiles, each with 10 warheads which could destroy 160 targets—more targets than there are cities in the Soviet Union." A Trident submarine dives into the oceans of the world with 24 missiles aboard able to destroy 500 separate targets.

But the Soviets, notes the *Los Angeles Times*, have titanic nuclear submarines—behemoths almost as big as the American Essex-class aircraft carrier—with a displacement of 30,000 tons, equipped with 20 tubes for ballistic missiles that have a range of 4,000 miles. According to *Chemical and Engineering News* the Soviets, based on U.S. Defense Department reports, have 78% of the land-based missiles—5,500 warheads compared to 2,152 for the Americans. Currently in Europe, "the Soviets have a 6-1 advantage," helped by deployment so far of 480 triple-headed SS-20s, to which Mikhail Gorbachev has now added the deployment of SS-22s.

We no longer need to wonder at the credibility of Revelation 8:8 and 9, where we read that a terrible "burning with fire was cast into the sea" and "the third part of the creatures which were in the sea, and had life, died; and the third part of the ships were destroyed." Dr. Carl Sagan goes on network TV in late 1984 to insist that it is the current consensus of nuclear physicists (15,000 consultants) that it would only take 100 of the existing 63,000 nuclear bombs to plunge the northern hemisphere into nuclear winter. There would occur the death of one-third of mankind with the descent of night around the clock and a drop of temperatures by 70 degrees Fahrenheit. The Bible predicts this scenario in many prophetic passages, including Matthew 24:29, where Jesus assured that during the "tribulation of those days shall the sun be darkened, and the moon shall not give her light."

One would do well to ask how many nations currently have nuclear bombs. Writes Jack Cahill in the *Toronto Star*, "Forty-four countries of the world already have the capability to detonate a nuclear device, and the ever-increasing number is causing grave concern to military analysts and disarmament experts." According to the International Atomic Energy Agency, as cited in the *New York Times*, fifty nations are currently jockeying, dabbling and dancing on the fringes of the nuclear club. France has jumped up its expenditures in this area by 17.6% this year over last and, like Britain and Canada, provides nuclear reactors for Third World countries around the world. It now has to be conceded that the Israelis knew very well what they were doing when they bombed out the Iraqi reactor in 1981—the Iraqis were doubtless intending to develop bombs with which to destroy the state of Israel. Canada's Candu Reactor, of course, provided India with know-how to produce its first nuclear bomb which it felt it had to have to match Red

China. The *New China News Agency* crows that Red China has taken a giant leap forward (or backward) by currently going into the mass production of "both strategic and tactical missiles." Presently, it has some 300 nuclear warheads. Although playing its cards extremely close to the chest, Israel let it be known thirteen years ago at the time of the Yom Kippur War that she had thirteen nuclear bombs assembled and emplaned. The *Jerusalem Post* reports forty new nuclear bombs being mounted on missiles around Jericho. In all, it has more than 200 nuclear bombs in readiness; I personally saw some of them in 1983. In addition to South Africa's nuclear arsenal (CBS Evening News), a host of nations, like Pakistan, Libya, Brazil, and Argentina, are at least on the verge of joining the nuclear club. "If we had had the atomic bomb [rigged and ready]," grumbled an Argentine authority, "the British fleet would not have begun its war in the Atlantic [the Falklands]."

Steve Weissman and Herbert Krosney's new book, *The Islamic Bomb,* makes frightening reading, reasoning that what the forty nations of Islam are saying with their vast oil fortunes is, " 'Nice Doggie!' until you can find a rock. Then when you can get your hand on that ultimate nuclear weapon, you turn and deal with that teethy growl in whatever way you feel is in your own best interests!"

In addition to the possibility that the Gaddafis, the Khomeinis, or the Colonel Mariams might use nuclear blackmail, is the fear of nuclear "accidents" or "miscalculations." If the Soviets had nuclear accidents—if, say, one of their submarines would run aground off the North Atlantic coast, like their nuclear submarine which beached on Swedish shores in 1981—would such an accident trigger an all-out nuclear war? That's surely one of the world's "heavies"! We do know that the American Pentagon admits to having had some thirty-two serious nuclear accidents, the more open-mouthed Center for Defense Information in Washington insisting there have been at least ninety-six. I was close to one near Cambridge, England, when a B-47 bomber crashed into a nuclear bomb storage center. Only some kind of "miracle" prevented a nuclear blast 1800 times more powerful than that suffered by Hiroshima—the accident would have killed perhaps 20 million and "a large part of eastern England would now be a desert." An even closer call occurred when "a crashing B-52 bomber jettisoned two nuclear bombs over Goldsboro, North Carolina. A parachute deployed on one bomb, while the other broke apart on impact. The parachute cords of the first bomb caught in a tree, and five of the six interlocking safety switches were released when the bomb jolted. Only one switch prevented the explosion of a 24-megaton bomb, 1800 times more powerful than the one dropped on Hiroshima in 1945. The Pentagon immediately bought all the farmland in the area where the second bomb broke apart, but they never have been able to find all the pieces."

When one reads such accounts in the press, one cannot but turn to the Bible to such prophecies of the last days as that found in Joel 2:3: "A fire devoureth before them; and behind them a flame burneth . . . [into] desolate wilderness; yea, and nothing shall escape"; or again, "The fire hath devoured the pastures of the wilderness, and the flame hath burned all the trees of the field" (Joel 1:19). Isaiah makes the broader expression that "the inhabitants of the earth are burned, and few men left" (24:6). Perhaps the most serious nuclear accident to hit the publicity fan was the "Three-Mile Island" incident in Pennsylvania in 1978. There is still a highly volatile argument about how far the meltdown got, how much radioactivity escaped, and how close the accident came to taking the northeastern United States to the brink of a nuclear inferno.

This discussion leads us to state that, among the proliferating "kinds" as well as "degrees" of new fires being invented by scientists, the neutron bomb has come to world attention in the eighties. President Carter put plans for this bomb on hold, but President Reagan and President Mitterand of France have decided to go ahead and manufacture these bombs in large numbers. They are "designed to produce far more radiation and far less blast and heat than other tactical nuclear weapons, so that they kill people without severe damage to their surroundings" (*New York Times*). Some scientists have observed that Zechariah 14:12 is a precise description of the effects of the neutron bomb: "Their flesh shall consume away while they stand . . . and their tongue shall consume away in their mouth." The *Globe and Mail* editorializes that the decision to go ahead with the neutron bomb was the biggest step taken toward "Armageddon" since 1961. Why? Because, according to the editorial, this decision augured "theater" war—and, of course, this was the triggering issue which produced the huge "peace" marches in Western Europe.

It is contended by President Reagan's network of intelligence forces that the Soviets, for all their cosmetic peace propaganda, are indeed making ready for picking off Afghanistan and for making further forays into Europe, and that they are preparing for nuclear theater war involving surgical thrusts. For while they talk peace, their military postures worldwide are poised for offense, not defense. At home the Soviets are spending sixteen times as much as the Americans on civil defense—for provisions such as bomb shelters, indicating that they seriously entertain "the hope not only of surviving but, indeed, winning nuclear war against the United States" (*Los Angeles Times*).

In Europe, there is a Catch-22 situation. According to Dan Rather in his prime-time series "CBS Reports" there are 7,000 nuclear warheads in West Germany; and to a people well aware of the terrible ravages of war, this could spell doom. The neutron bomb strikes fear because it makes a regional nuclear war more possible. And, as is almost universally felt, who—or what—would indicate that this would not escalate into World War III? A *Reuter* report states, "The North Atlantic Treaty Organization's arsenal of conventional anti-tank weapons is so deficient that it makes early recourse to nuclear weapons . . . more likely, otherwise a Soviet attack would be absolutely devastating."

Then there is the matter of chemical warfare. It is a widely publicized fact that Iraq engaged this horrific weapon against Iran in 1985, and it seems now to be reasonably well-proven that the Soviets have a huge arsenal of chemical warfare weapons. And, despite the fact that they were outlawed by an international agreement in 1925, Soviet agents used them in Cambodia and Laos. According to a U.S. State Department report, "The death toll from so-called 'Yellow Rain' and other chemical weapons was 6,310 in Laos, 981 in Cambodia, and 3,042 in Afghanistan." The U.S. Secretary of State states "firmly that the United States has evidence the outlawed weapons were used in Afghanistan and Laos." Harvard's molecular biologist Matthew Meselson revealed at the Washington Conference of the American Association for the Advancement of Science "that the United States had more than 100,000 poison gas artillery shells," while Professor Arthur Westling remarked that, with the Soviets' conduct and the recrudescence of "interest in producing chemical weapons, the world finds itself on the threshold of a chemical arms race" (*Toronto Star*). President Reagan has announced publicly that after a thirteen-year halt the U.S. is openly resuming "the manufacture of two new chemical binary weapons." A whole section of the Washington Conference was given over to a discussion of biological warfare. I was riding on a plane with a Jewish government official recently. He assured me that the simplest way to destroy the population of a continent in a matter of two or three days is with biological or bacteriological warfare. He contended that the technology for this is so sophisticated and so ready that either of the Americas—or both—or Eurasia could have their total populations exterminated in less than a week. It needs to be kept in mind that Jesus predicted not only "famines" but "pestilences" (Matthew 24:7).

Another means of wreaking holocaust on humanity (to which we have not yet alluded) is the laser beam. The term LASER stands for "Light Amplification by Stimulated Emission of Radiation." Lasers are incredibly powerful instruments and they have a variety of constructive uses. A laser concentrates tremendous energy into a pinpoint of light and generates intense heat. Metals can be welded by it, machine guns and rockets fired by it. In medicine, laser beams are sent through glass fibers to treat growths in inaccessible parts of the body, and detached retinas are rejoined to the eye by their use. Laser beams are being used in space communication to bring television pictures from outer space in seconds; and in industry they have vaporized coal into gas, making hitherto uneconomical coal seams workable. For purposes of destruction they can be mounted on jets and satellites and have already been used "to knock airplanes from the sky." Huge lasers, it is envisaged, can be placed "in space to shoot at enemy missiles coming up through the atmosphere." As early as in 1982 a British scientist was writing of the evolving capacity of the Soviets to function from "fortresses" in outer space. From such a vantage point they could paralyze the U.S. intercontinental missile installations using laser beams. It was as a result of this fear that President Reagan announced his "Star Wars" venture: that through the use of the laser the U.S. proposed to build a "Protection Shield" ("Fortress America") whereby the Soviet ICBMs would be zapped by the U.S. lasers in the sky as soon as they came out of their silos. Robert Waters writes, "A space-based laser beam mirror [is envisaged by the U.S. State Department, a weapon] capable of destroying Soviet nuclear missiles up to 5,000 miles away in outer space."

Aviation Week and Space Technology claims that "the Soviet Union has a new killer satellite in earth orbit capable of destroying several orbiting U.S. satellites. It's an anti-satellite battle station equipped with clusters of infrared-homing guided interceptors that could destroy multiple U.S. spacecraft. The podded miniature attack vehicles provide a new U.S.S.R. capability for a sneak attack on U.S. satellites." Robert Moss writes of all this in his new book, *Death Beam*.

Gerald Utting argues that the first battle of the future world war is likely to be fought in outer space by robot-controlled satellites using long-range missiles and lasers. The aim? To "blind" the other side to a surprise attack, to gain perhaps a couple of minutes during which an enemy would have to guess what an aggressor was doing with his intercontinental missile strike force. Utting quotes *Avaiation Week and Space Technology* that we can now be sure that the Soviets have succeeded with breakneck speed in having "developed a new and much more sophisticated variety of sputnik that makes a war in which satellite kills satellite much more possible."

Another catastrophic scenario was recently pointed out by Val Sears, science editor of the *Toronto Star,* in a feature article quoting German scientists: "On the day the world ends, a Soviet Cosmos satellite—supposedly on its routine picture-taking mission—is crossing the United States at a height of about 450 kilometers. Suddenly over the Great Plains, a few pounds of enriched plutonium in the fake satellite explode, blanketing the United States and Canada with a shower of gamma rays. In one-billionth of a second all electrical power and transmissions in North America are blanked out. Cars, trucks, and machinery stop. Nuclear power plants go dark. Radio and television stations go off the air. Planes crash. Missile systems fail, and, in any case, the President of the United States has no way to communicate with the silo crews and set the missiles off on a retaliatory strike. This effect is called a Nuclear Electromagnetic Pulse, and even in an age of increasingly horrifying weapons, it is giving the Pentagon and NATO nightmares. The prestigious German newspaper *Die Zeit* recently devoted two pages to a description of this satanic weapon that can cripple the total nervous system of civilization. American scientific and military journals are paying more and more attention to a doomsday scenario that begins with a Nuclear Electromagnetic Pulse. *Science* magazine recently ran three articles on it in a row." Val Sears sums up, "The 'Satanic' nuclear pulse has made it peace [or] Doomsday."

Were I not a Christian, I simply do not know what posture I would adopt in the face of the overwhelming odds against the human race. I sympathize with Dr. Frank Somers of the University of Toronto medical faculty, who insists that man is on a direct collision course with nuclear annihilation. He feels that we must escalate the grassroots support for all disarmament agitation. Margo Raudsepp, in conceding the same—that man is currently headed straight for doomsday—says that "we must all get angry and take out our righteous indignation on the leaders of the world, by insisting they make love, not war." Frank Showler of the Canadian Friends Service Committee affirms, "We do not believe that the way to peace is to prepare for war." (William F. Buckley insists on the reverse, that "the way to peace *is* to prepare for war.") Everyone supposedly yearns for peace, yet we are all drifting straight into the barracuda jaws of war.

I have no personal doubt about what a Christian is to do and think. He is to seek peace and make peace—whenever and wherever he can. But he must always remain aware that Jesus prophesied that man is headed for war—terrible, but not terminal, war. There is hope, blessed hope! Man would burn himself up, but for the advent of Christ. Dealing with this theme, St. Peter writes, "The Lord is not slack concerning his promise, as some men count slackness; but is longsuffering to us-ward, not willing that any should perish, but that all should come to repentance" (2 Peter 3:9). St. Jude urges, "Save [them] with fear, pulling them out of the fire" (Jude 23). And St. Paul wrote to the Thessalonians, "To you who are troubled rest with us, when the Lord Jesus shall be revealed from heaven with his mighty angels, in flaming fire taking vengeance on them that know not God, and that obey not the gospel of our Lord Jesus Christ; who shall be punished with everlasting destruction from the presence of the Lord, and from the glory of his power" (2 Thessalonians 1:7-9). These are strong words.

Chapter Three

Society and
the Coming Christ

Jesus, in depicting the scenario leading up to His return, described how society at that time will be characterized. There will be a fresh outbreak of the social sins and moral depravities that dominated ancient Sodom and Gomorrah in Lot's time or the even more ancient civilization of Noah's day when man had degenerated into such moral depravity that "God saw that the wickedness of man was great in the earth, and that every imagination of the thoughts of his heart was only evil continually" (Gen. 6:5 KJV). Jesus foretold that "as it was in Noah's day, so will it also be in the days of the Son of man. People were eating and drinking, marrying wives and husbands, right up to the day Noah went into the ark, and the Flood came and destroyed them all. It will be the same as it was in Lot's day: people were eating and drinking, buying and selling, planting and building, but the day Lot left Sodom, God rained fire and brimstone from heaven and destroyed them all. It will be the same when the day comes for the Son of man to be revealed" (Luke 17:26-30 JB).

On every hand, writers are stating that society has gone sour and civilization is sick. As the Jewish pundit Mark Gayn reflected in the United Nations in New York, "Even more dangerous than the loss of world influence has been the decline of moral standards in the West." Pope John Paul II reckons that society worldwide is in the throes of "unprecedented change"; that "everyone has the impression of being dragged away and overcome by an irresistible current . . . seized by frenzy.'' Sir Cyril Black, the distinguished British M.P., pleads that all law-abiding citizens combine to "slam on the brakes on a sick society.'' Writing on this current sickness, Harold Lindsell, former editor of *Christianity Today,* points out that "this present world is doomed. The scent of death is upon it. It is committing suicide and nothing can save it . . . until the coming of Jesus Christ.'' The Bible forecasts the state of society at the time of Christ's second coming: a maelstrom of lawlessness; a hurricane of violence; a tornado of selfishness; a cyclone of sexual incontinence; a typhoon of revolt against the tried, traditional structures of society. Upheaval and chaos will threaten order and serenity of any kind.

Possibly it is the fact of man's being so incognito, living in limbo, and flung into the rat race of life which leads toward his becoming so selfish and egocentric. Is this not precisely as St. Paul predicted? "In the last days the times will be full of danger. Men will become utterly self-centered . . . loving all the time what gives them pleasure'' (2 Timothy 3:1,2,4, Phillips). "There will come in the last days mockers who live according to their own godless desires . . . men who complain and curse their fate while trying all the time to mold life according to their own desires. They 'talk big' but will pay men great respect if it is to their own advantage'' (Jude 18, 16, Phillips). An Australian legislator pays a visit to Britain and returns completely disillusioned, commenting, "England is lost in a sargasso sea of sex, sadism and psychedelics.'' And CBS advertises the showing of the film *The World, the Flesh, and the Devil,* assuring viewers that it will "really turn you on,'' as if getting oneself turned on is the chief end of living.

Undoubtedly, sex is the social area where moral degeneration shows up most sharply. "In the last days,'' wrote St. Paul, people will be "incontinent, . . . intemperate, . . . utterly lacking in purity,'' while "seducers shall wax worse and worse.'' Jesus portended that pressure would be brought to bear "to seduce, if it were possible, even the elect. But take ye heed: behold, I have foretold you all things'' (Mark 13:22,23). St. Peter presaged how men in society would "make of sensual lusts and debauchery a bait to catch those who have barely begun to escape from their heathen environment. They promise them freedom, but are themselves slaves of corruption; for a man is the slave of whatever has mastered him" (2 Peter 2:18,19 NEB).

The whole swing of public communications is toward what the protagonists of a sexually permissive and completely promiscuous attitude toward life call "the open society." In the words of a *Time* cover story, ours is the era of "The Sex Explosion." So *Playboy* becomes the most read, or, should we say, gazed at, magazine on the continent. Literature professor Lord Elton of Oxford claims that eighty-three percent of the modern novel centers on perverting Judeo-Christian moral laws. Another English educator once said to me that, however sophisticated much modern writing is, one would think that those who produced much of it were living in a sewer. Is it any wonder that Jude forecasts, "Their dreams lead them to defile"? Jude linked dreams and sexual promiscuity long before that other Jewish seer, Sigmund Freud, appeared on the scene.

Time tells us of sex emporiums being built "to view the copulation"—live and in color—as next in the hedonists' plans for the future. It also describes how, a few blocks from Times Square, "couples cavort in the nude and simulate intercourse" while cameramen are shooting. Add to this the Home Box Office pay-TV programming and the TV cassettes which bring any variety of sex films into homes around the world.

Obsession with sex leads to a recrudescence of nudity. St. John could well have been writing of this when he indicated, "You have no eyes to see that you are . . . naked" (Revelation 3:17, Phillips). St. Peter indicated that men's eyes would indeed be occupied, however, as he foresaw swingers "reveling in their dissipation, carousing with you. They have eyes full of adultery, insatiable for sin" (2 Peter 2:13,14 RSV).

The columnist Sydney Katz foresees the society of the future in which females will wear nothing but a bit of translucent paint to accentuate their features, with a heavy spray of transparent foam over their bodies to insulate them from the discomforts which weather conditions impose, but not from the voluptuous gaze of depraved males. It seems ironic that in Nairobi, Kenya, the minister of education had to appeal to teachers from the West who come to Kenya to refrain from wearing miniskirts and other sparse dress. After all, it was Anglo-Americans (he meant, of course, the Christian missionaries), who had taught the Africans the virtues of concealing nakedness. And now he hoped they would not come out and undo the good which they had done in generations past.

This inordinate preoccupation with sex leads to gross and shameless immorality, both premarital and extramarital, its proportions today a sign that Christ must come back and right this wrong. St. Paul anticipated that in the final age of this world promiscuity would reach unprecedented proportions with "passionate and unprincipled" people who would "worm their way into people's houses, and find easy prey in silly women with an exaggerated sense of sin and morbid cravings" (2 Timothy 3:3,6,7, Phillips). Jesus forewarned that, as in Noah's day, along with their "eating and drinking," people would be "marrying and giving in marriage" (Matthew 24:38), the implication being that they will focus on marriage after marriage to the extent that they ignore spiritual and moral laws. In the Revelation of Jesus Christ, St. John forecast that "her sins are piled high as heaven" (Revelation 18:5 NEB).

Reader's Digest claims that ninety-eight percent of Swedes engage in premarital intercourse and the average man over thirty years of age has, or has had, seven sex partners; already the average for those between eighteen and thirty is eight partners. A reporter from Russia writes in the *New Zealand Herald* that nearly all Russians have premarital relations. The average city girl in Russia has had "several abortions before marriage," these being legal and free. And the divorce rate in Russia, according to the United Nations, is nearly equal to that of the United States. *Newsweek* assesses that Western morals have dipped more in the last ten years than in the previous fifty years and when *Time's* cover story was "The Adulterous Generation," one did not have to read far to realize how fast the skid downward is moving. In a single year in Britain, for example, there was an eight percent increase in the number of divorces granted. In 1870 there were 10,000 divorces in the United States. In 1984 there were more than a million. Add to this the two million abortions, and you realize the poor state of our personal morality.

The moral depravity which the Scriptures indicate God hates most is sexual deviation and perversion, including homosexuality. Both St. Jude and St. Peter foresaw that there would exist a society which paralleled that of Sodom and Gomorrah in this respect. These were the sins of those ancient twin cities of iniquity. Before the Lord comes, wrote St. Jude, society would sink to the level of "Sodom and Gomorrah and the adjacent cities who . . . gave themselves up to sexual immorality and perversion" (Jude 7, Phillips). Whole novels and films are today centering on the theme of homosexuality. The late Richard Burton tells how repugnant it was for him and Rex Harrison to play the roles of homosexuals. However, it is the way to make a quick buck; hence, it becomes the theme of stage plays like *The Boys in the Band*. The title of an article in the *National Enquirer* is "The New People: Desexualization in American Life," and the big fad in clothes is "unisex." A prominent physician was quoted as assessing that there are 100,000 homosexuals in Metro-Toronto, and a radio newscast announced that, of Holland's population of 15 million, five percent are homosexuals. If Toronto and Holland have five percent homosexuality, it is probably a fair estimate to state that five percent of Europeans and North Americans are homosexual. God, who created man "male and female," needs to come back and sort out His creation, and He has promised that He will.

More and more, sexual perversion is on the increase. *Reader's Digest* asserts that increasing numbers of books are making no reference whatsoever to natural sex relations. In place of normal heterosexual activity, there are sex-incited flagellations, sexual deviations, sadism, masochism, torture, and even murder: every conceivable form of sexual deviation and perversion which the depraved imagination can concoct.

Then there is the current worldwide pandemic of venereal diseases. We are informed that currently in Africa as much as 40 percent of the child-bearing women have venereal disease. In Sweden, sometimes called the "first of the enlightened countries" where "the new morality" has been pioneered, venereal disease has shot up 750 percent over the last twelve years. Ottawa reports a 30 percent increase in venereal disease in one year and in the United States, in a year, gonorrhea increased 21 percent. Of the 2.5 million Americans who presently have gonorrhea, it is estimated that 800,000 of these are women who do not yet know they have it. Meanwhile, they are passing it on to their sex partners.

Chatelaine magazine tells us that venereal disease has doubled in Canada during the last decade and that most of the new cases strike those between the ages of fifteen and twenty-four. In fact, venereal disease has already become a plague. Imagine what will happen during what Jesus called the "Great Tribulation," when there will be acute shortages of medicines, and death will be all around. The normal restraints in society will all be disrupted, people will be in distress such as man has never known before, and the Church of Jesus Christ will be gone. Promiscuous sex will undoubtedly be engaged in, without inhibitions, and the inevitable result will be a wild pandemic of venereal disease.

The National Center for Disease Control of the United States has apprised the public through such magazines as *Time* of the rising incidence of "herpes simplex two." Dr. Marion Powell warns, "Herpes has become an epidemic in North America. It is estimated that 50 million people have herpes infection." Ann Landers apprises her 82 million daily readers, "We now have a form of V.D.—herpes simplex II—for which there is no cure."

Jesus warned His disciples that a sure sign of His return and the end of the age would be an uncontrollable outbreak of "epidemics" (and it was St. Luke, the Greek physician, who recorded this particular word "loimos"—Luke 21:11 LB). *Time* confirms the stark truth of Jesus' word of prophecy that "epidemics" would proliferate prior to His return by quoting eminent Dr. Lewis Thomas, noted biologist and prize-winning author (*The Lives of a Cell*), "Just a few years ago, in an excess of hubris, I predicted we were nearly finished with the problem of infection. I take it back." It also quotes Dr. William Foege, Director of Atlanta's (peerless) Centers for Disease Control, "I fully anticipate that possibly in our lifetime, we will see another flu strain that is as deadly as 1918. We have not figured out good ways to counter that."

"Epidemics" is the word used some twenty times in *Time*'s cover story (a nine-pager: July 4, 1983). The particular epidemic which is highlighted is AIDS (Acquired Immune Deficiency Syndrome), of which U.S. Secretary of Health and Human Services Dr. Margaret Heckler assesses, "AIDS is our No. 1 health concern and the epidemic is our No. 1 priority." Who is affected chiefly by AIDS? "Drug users and active homosexuals

[who] are continually bombarded by a gallery of illnesses." In this epidemic of AIDS: "So far, 75.9% of the victims in North America have been homosexual men, 15% intravenous drug users, 5% immigrants from Haiti, and 1% hemophiliacs. More than 90% of the victims are males between the ages of 20 and 49." Is the homosexual community jolted? Yes, they complain, "We're treated like lepers." Nurses "quit rather than deal with AIDS cases. Half of the dentists in San Francisco now wear some protective covering, usually rubber gloves while treating [suspected homosexuals]. There's no way around it. According to the American Dental Association, gloves are not enough. Its council on central therapeutics recommends that dentists and their assistants wear masks and eye coverings as well, while treating their patients." *Time* goes on, "Homosexuals should be banned from all food-handling jobs. Undertakers are wary of handling AIDS victims. The Red Cross, which collects about half of the 12 million units of blood given each year, now excludes 'all sexually active homosexuals.' " One finds it quite amazing that "New York City's trendy, leftist *Village Voice* " does not hesitate to warn its homosexual readership, " 'It's suicidal to go to the baths.' " Yes, the terrible scourge has indeed got to the homosexuals themselves. "Says Craig Rowland, 34, 'You're always looking at a potential partner and thinking, "Is this the one to kill me?" ' "

I was disappointed that *Time* made no reference to the churches which are blatantly considering—or already are—ordaining active homosexual "clergymen." Surely, when *Time* sighs there's "no cure" even though "nothing in the history of disease detection compares in size or intensity with the chase now under way to solve the mystery of AIDS"—and with the Red Cross reporting "a 15.1% slump in blood collections"—surely churches could call a halt to any endorsement whatsoever on active homosexuality.

Homosexuality is devastating to the institution of Christian marriage. Is it any wonder, then, that St. Paul foresees that, as "God's Spirit specifically tells us" . . . there be those who "forbid marriage" (1 Timothy 4:1, 3, Phillips)! Youth gods Mick Jagger of the Rolling Stones and the late John Lennon of the Beatles went on record to state their opinion that legal marriage was obsolete. A national magazine in the United States advertises a celebrity whose vaunted opinion is, "I'd rather be Dead than Wed." Too often, these are the modern role models the masses aspire to follow.

The casting to the winds of the moral law of God means that children refuse to heed their parents. In an increasingly large number of instances they either don't know who their parents are, or are not brought up by them at all. Is it surprising then, that St. Paul foretold "the last days," in which children would be "disobedient to their parents" (2 Timothy 3:1,2 RSV). Jesus forewarned His disciples who wanted to know when He would return, that one of the phenomena would be that "children will turn against their parents" (Matthew 10:21 NEB).

A newspaper reports that, in a London school, five-to-seven-year-olds were so completely out of hand that John Silkin, a member of Parliament, assessed: "The problem is so serious that the staff are leaving through fear of mental and physical breakdown." Razor blade slashings and hangings were reported. A West Coast judge has stated that he would like to write a book called *I Hate Parents!* He is convinced that the reason for juvenile delinquency is parental profligacy.

With society in such a critical state, why are the majority not aware of their peril, and why do they not repent? Because, as St. Paul foresaw, "In the last days . . . men shall be . . . despisers of those that are good" (2 Timothy 3:3). We may be amazed by the fact that, when an Ontario university opened, the freshmen were initiated by the sophomores, who led them up and down the corridors (allegedly of both the dormitories and the academic halls) shouting "Jesus Christ" several times over. And this was followed by an unrepeatable chain of expletives and four-letter words. Why does this happen? Because the "outlook of the lower nature is enmity with God; it is not subject to the law of God" (Romans 8:7). Wrote St. Paul to the Romans, "Every person must submit to the supreme authorities. There is no authority but by act of God, and the existing authorities are instituted by him; consequently anyone who rebels against authority is resisting a divine institution, and those who so resist have themselves to thank for the punishment they will receive. For government, a terror to crime, has no terrors for good behavior" (Romans 13:1-3 NEB).

St. Peter made it very plain that prior to the Day of Judgment there will be "those who have indulged all the foulness of their lower natures, and have nothing but contempt for authority. . . . These men, with no more sense than the unreasoning brute beasts . . . delight in daylight self-indulgence; . . . and with their high-sounding nonsense they use the sensual pull of the lower passions to attract those who were just on the point of cutting loose from their companions in misconduct" (2 Peter 2:10,12,13,18, Phillips).

Organized crime is currently doing a $100 billion a year fleecing job on North Americans. In Britain, crime has doubled in a decade, and, according to a newspaper article, juvenile crime arrests in France have gone up 900 percent during the same period. Law enforcement agencies are being beefed up and reorganized. The non-lethal weaponry expenditure in the United States is up 1,200 percent. But can they stem the tidal wave? Even the young are concerned. "What is this world coming to?" writes a teenager to Ann Landers. "It seems the only place one is safe anymore, is in his grave."

Since they were both Jews, Paul and Peter might specifically have had Israel in mind while writing of the conditions which would prevail throughout the world at the time of Christ's coming. Crime in Israel, according to *Time*, "is soaring to levels that upright Israel has never known. In greater Tel Aviv (pop. 800,000), robberies are up 125% in a year, murders have doubled, purse snatchers have become common, and 400 prostitutes are on the street." The true Christian should not give up on social action. He is not looking for an excavation in the cemetery in which to bury a degenerated society, but anticipates elevation to the skies. With this expectation he can strive for reform in a deteriorating society without capitulating to despair.

What has now begun to typify lawless acts is violence, yet another sure sign that the Prince of Peace must come again. "The earth also was corrupt before God, and the earth was filled with violence" was Moses' description of social conditions in Noah's day. "And God said unto Noah, the end of all flesh is come before me; for the earth is filled with violence" (Genesis 6:11,13). Declared our Lord, "As things were in Noah's days, so will they be when the Son of man comes."

"Violence—physical violence, physical intimidation," says the U.S. president, "is seemingly an accepted form of opinion-forming in today's world." The *Wall Street Journal* reckons human society is "sick and frighteningly violent." "The instinct for violence," sighs Arthur Schlesinger, Jr., "is almost as if a primal curse has been fixed on our nation. We are a violent people." "Violence . . . terrorism and reprisal," laments the pope, "send a painful quiver through the entire body of mankind." "Our boring lives lead to violence," reckons psychologist Erich Fromm. "Even the churches now encourage violence," laments *Time*.

What is it that has gone wrong with man? St. Paul wrote to Timothy that "God's Spirit specifically tells us that in later days there will be men . . . whose consciences are as dead as seared flesh" (1 Timothy 4:1,2, Phillips). To quote Robert Ardrey: "Man is by inerasable nature as aggressive as an animal." The late Marshall McLuhan forecast that the whole mentality of the rising generation is being brainwashed by television, and no one really knows where this road is taking us. By the time a youth graduates from high school, he has, on the average, seen 18,000 hours of TV, which is 7,000 hours more than he has been in school. And what is really tragic: he has seen 17,000 killings of fellow human beings.

The Scriptures also assure us that before Christ returns there will be drunkenness. Alcohol is now North America's third greatest killer, following heart disease and cancer. According to WLS radio, sixty-one percent of fatal automobile accidents are caused by liquor; in France, it is sixty-six percent. Italy is "the world's No. 1 alcohol consumer." Currently, ten million North Americans are alcoholics, and the cost of liquor to employers through absenteeism and inefficiency is a staggering statistic.

Ann Landers' column describes the torment inflicted on a home by a drunken father: "People who live with the screaming, beating, broken glass, black eyes, knocked-out teeth, police at the door, bill collectors, the whole ugly bit," are aware that there is a price which goes with alcoholism. The Ann Landers' column also indicates that, with one North American in four suffering from some form of mental imbalance, a third of these are alcohol-related. Forty percent of the Frenchmen in mental institutions are alcoholics. Here again is where Christ's coming again is so practical. It gives hope and assurance that ultimately our Lord is coming again to institute a redeemed society.

Jesus prophesied that before His return and the end of the age, society would be hit with pestilences. This refers to the rampaging communal ravages across the world. We are told that in Canada, with a population of only 24 million, a million people have lung cancer at some stage of development due to the excesses of cigarette smoking, and that, unless some other disease gets in ahead, it will eventually kill every one of its victims. Each cigarette a heavy smoker lights cuts an average of fifteen minutes off his life (see *Toronto Star*, Dec. 11, 1984). Ann Landers reckons that 50 million Americans will eventually capitulate to cancer unless a cure is found.

The *Australian* affirms that cigarette smokers are ten times more likely to die of lung cancer; six times more likely to die of bronchitis and emphysema; three times more likely to have a heart attack; much more likely to get cancer of the larynx, esophagus, and bladder; to have unsuccessful pregnancies; and to have such misfortunes as car accidents. On the average, smokers have one-third more illnesses than non-smokers and live eight years less. But all the warnings have altogether too little effect, for the annual increase of cigarettes sold worldwide continues at the rate of 70 billion more each year.

Another worldwide Satanic pestilence is "drugs." "When you follow your own wrong inclination, your lives will produce evil results,"wrote St. Paul to the Galatians. One of these results is "spiritism"—also translated "witchcraft" and "sorcery." The word comes from the same Greek root as "pharmacy," referring to the use of pharmaceutical drugs to induce psychic reactions. In the Revelation of Jesus Christ (16:13-16) it is clear that what is going to motivate, mobilize, and march the leaders and the armies of the world to Armageddon is demonization, induced by the massive use of drugs. Fifty-six percent of North American teenagers have experimented with marijuana, an increasing number making it a regular habit. Hard drugs, especially heroin, are tragically on the rise. In England the newspapers in 1984 were filled with accounts of how heroin had doubled within one year. But the drug which has attacked the middle class most extensively is cocaine. "The Phil Donahue Show" (Dec. 11, 1984) gave the statistics that 22 million North Americans are currently smoking, snorting or freebasing coke; that the habit is costing them 34 billion dollars annually—all illegal; and that 81% of the users are utterly unable, regardless of how hard they try, to kick the habit.

An equally frightening pestilence of our time is pollution. Until the seventies few of us had ever heard of the word "ecology". Now most sixth-graders can tell you not only its meaning, but also that, before the century is out, the pollution of our whole physical environment will be such that the human race will be suffocated or poisoned to death. *Christianity Today* carries an interview with an ecology expert who insists that the suffocation of man by atmospheric, land, water, and food pollutants is an inexorable threat demanding immediate remedy or sure doom. A TV satirist pictures New Yorkers staring up through the street smog and trying to identify what a dim midday light was; suddenly an oldtimer calls on his memory to reckon that it could be the sun. Someone has suggested that ours is "a technological society which underwent biological disintegration for a lack of ecological understanding." And so to the list of scientific and technological inventions for the potential annihilation of man is added extermination from overpowering pollution. But Jesus Christ will come again to cope with pollution.

The projection of selfishness is covetousness. The apostles Peter, Paul, Jude, James and John all predicted that greed would be a characteristic of the times immediately preceding the return of Christ. "In their greed for money they will trade on your credulity with sheer fabrication," forecast St. Peter, adding that they will be "past masters in mercenary greed" (2 Peter 2:3,14 NEB). Before the Lord comes, indicated St. Jude, some men would stoop to follow "error for pay" (Jude 11 NEB). "In an age that is near its close," projected St. James, certain men will "have piled up wealth" (James 5:3 NEB). Uncaring and unsparing in their exploitations, James charged, "The wages you never paid to the men who mowed your fields are loud against you, and the outcry of the reapers has reached the ears of the Lord of Hosts. You have lived on earth in wanton luxury, fattening yourselves like cattle—and the day for slaughter has come. You have condemned the innocent and murdered him; he offers no resistance. . . . To you who have great possessions: weep and wail over the miserable fate descending on you. Your riches have rotted; your fine clothes are moth-eaten; your silver and gold have rusted away, and their very rust will be evidence against you and consume your flesh like fire" (James 5:4-6,1-3 NEB).

St. John predicted in his Revelation of Jesus Christ that the smug rich would boast, "I am rich, I have prospered, and there is nothing that I need [not knowing that he was] pitiable . . . and . . . poverty stricken" (Revelation 3:17, Phillips). The mad pursuit of materialism can be seen in bestsellers like Adam Smith's *The Money Game,* Lundberg's *The Rich and the Super Rich,* Cameron Hawley's *Executive Suite*, Morton Shulman's *Anyone Can Make a Million,* and Louis Auchincloss' *The Guilty Ones*. These deify the glories of being rich. The fact that each year in North America a thousand millionaires commit suicide gives evidence of the fact that money in itself is not a passport to happiness. One opens the newspapers and magazines, or looks at television, or turns on the radio in 1984 or 1985 to find a baseball pitcher being signed by the Atlanta Braves to a $60 million contract to pitch in relief. Boy George, or Prince, or Michael Jackson may gross an estimated $100 million out of a single concert tour or $40 million out of one album. The Jimi Hendrixes, the Janis Joplins, and the Elvis Presleys have said by their deaths as well as their lives—by their screamed emptiness, not their fullness—just how meaningless the existence of a modern hedonist really is. One of her closest friends laments of Elizabeth Taylor, the most glamorized actress of our generation, that ". . . there is about this lovely creature an inevitable sadness, a prescience of doom, the feeling that inevitably life is passing her by."

As for the communist world, its whole way of life is built on the crass materialist theory that "a man is what he eats." There has never in history been a political philosophy so undisguisedly based on sheer materialism as that of Marxism. As Winston Churchill said, "Everyone can see how Communism rots the soul of a nation, how it makes it hungry and abject indeed, and proves a base and abominable reward."

Gluttony, according to the American Medical Association, is currently a major hazard to good health in the United States. For those of us who have an abundance of material things, Jesus warned of a spate of overeating and drunkenness which would spread over the world. "In the time of the coming of the

Son of Man, life will be as it was in the days of Noah," apprised
Jesus, when "people ate and drank" (Luke 17:26,27, Phillips).
That would constitute the existence of multitudes: their contrived *raison d'être*. "Keep a watch on yourselves," our Lord
later forewarned those who at that time would be His followers.
"Do not let your minds be dulled by dissipation and drunkenness and worldly cares so that the great Day closes upon you
suddenly like a trap" (Luke 21:34 NEB). The late Max Lerner
concluded that "America is now living a Babylonian existence."
But whether one interprets the Babylon of Revelation 17 and 18
as a geographic area such as the Middle East rising on its oil
wealth, or an ecclesiastical organization, or the developed world
generally—one sees God's judgment about to be poured out as
the age bottoms out. "Babylon the great! [all] nations have
drunk of the wine [of] her fornication, . . . merchants of the
earth are waxed rich through the abundance of her delicacies.
[A] voice from heaven [said], come out of her, my people, that
ye be not partakers of her sins, [which] have reached unto
heaven, and God hath remembered her iniquities. . . . She hath
glorified herself, and lived deliciously—the merchandise of
gold, and silver, and precious stones, and of pearls, and fine
linen, and purple, and silk, and scarlet . . . vessels of most
precious wood, and of brass, and iron, and marble . . . [and]
wine, and oil, and fine flour . . . and horses, and chariots, and
slaves, and souls of men. [But alas] in one hour is thy judgment
come [when] she shall be utterly burned with fire: for strong is
the Lord God who judgeth her. [And those] who have committed fornication and lived deliciously with her, shall bewail her
and lament for her, when they shall see the smoke of her burning" (see Revelation 18:2-18). Those are not pleasant anticipa-
tions of a judgment which is yet to come: perhaps soon!

A present holocaust, which has doubtless been the news
story of 1984, is the famine in Africa. We in the West are the
wealthy of the earth wallowing in our surplusses and surfeiting.
We are the part of the world that spends a hundred million
dollars annually on reducing aids and diets, desperately trying
to stop eating, in stark and tragic contrast to the rest of the
human race who are trying just to get started: pathetic people to
whom a bowl of rice, a loaf of bread, or a piece of fish would be
like a moment in paradise!

When the disciples asked Jesus what would be the scenario at the time of His coming again and the end of the age, He replied that, insofar as people's intake of food and drink was concerned, "There will be famines . . . in different parts of the world" (Matthew 24:7, Phillips). In Revelation 6:5,6 (a passage used by a *Toronto Star* editorial to caption the tragic spread of famine over the earth) we see this same projected scene:"When the Lamb opened the third seal, I heard the third living creature say, 'Come!' I looked, and there before me was a black horse! Its rider was holding a pair of scales in his hand. Then I heard what sounded like a voice among the four living creatures saying, 'A quart of wheat for a day's wages, and do not damage the oil and the wine!' "

The black horse is symbolic of famine. In other Scriptures, such as Jeremiah 4:28 or Lamentations 4:8 and 9, black is associated with famine spreading over the land. In Revelation 6:8 we read that a killer famine will spread "over a fourth of the earth." Therefore, we can expect famine to spread in various places throughout the world. The black horse carries a rider who has a pair of scales in his hands—a symbol that apparently indicates careful rationing. It would take meticulous rationing indeed to distribute an income of a quart of wheat for a day's work! Certainly the breadwinner in any household would have all he or she could do to earn enough to feed one person, let alone a family. So the poverty in some parts of the world will verge on famine and in many places will lead to mass starvation.

Signs of the black horse of Revelation 6—of Jesus' warning that there will be famines in different parts of the world—are ubiquitous today. No one who believes in the return of Christ can see the countless pitifully starving people in the world today without sighing, "Even so, come, Lord Jesus!" (Rev. 22:20 KJV).

In June 1984, the second World Food Conference was held in Addis Ababa, Ethiopia. The U.N. had sponsored the World Food Council a decade earlier "to increase food production and rural agricultural development and eradicate hunger." But in 1984 "The news is grim. Hunger in the Third World [is] making a mockery of the 1974 World Food Conference's vow that within a decade no child would go to bed hungry, no family would fear for its next day's bread." Instead, and tragically, "estimates of the chronically hungry reach from 400 to 600 million . . . 150 million Africans face starvation in 24 nations" (*Toronto Star*, June 1984). Biologists Paul Erlich of Stanford University, William and Paul Paddock, and the late Sir Julian Huxley give great sections of the human race virtually no hope of avoiding the proliferating famine. Commenting gravely on the years immediately ahead, Erlich notes, "there is not the slightest hope of escaping a disastrous time of famines. . . . It is shockingly apparent that the battle to feed man will end in a rout." The Paddocks reckon that, from here on in, ". . . famines, greater than any in history, will ravage the underdeveloped nations!" The "CBS Evening News" calculates that currently 60 million humans starve to death annually in famines around the world—six times as many as those who starved to death in 1970. The World Food Conference in Rome estimates the current annual famine toll at 62 million. This amounts to 170,000 people every day of the year. That is comparable to all of the people of Regina starving to death in a 24-hour period, or all of the people of Vancouver in a week, or all of the people of Philadelphia in a month, or all of the people of the British Isles in a year—wiped out in all-voracious famine.

The World Council of Churches reckons, "The world is on a catastrophic course leading to mass starvation." Lee Griggs, *Time's* Nairobi bureau chief, spent eighteen months on a "terribly depressing" assignment: surveying the ravages of famine while traveling 15,000 miles. He said that "watching people die slowly from starvation is worse than watching them die quickly in war. The look of utter despair on their faces is something I'll never forget. . . . It's the children and babies your heart goes out to most, and to mothers who stare vacantly at you as they try to suckle babes at dried-up breasts."

Bob Hope came back from one of his safaris into areas of starvation remonstrating, "The scraps we toss in the garbage would be a sumptuous meal for them." Commenting on hunger in India, *Time* estimates that only half of India's 700 million people eat more than one meal a day. Tom Harpur writes from Africa that you have to see it to believe it—the conditions in which people in underdeveloped countries live. Eight hundred million of them, in addition to enduring hunger, have to cope with "living in squalid, dehumanizing shacks and camps." A

United Nations report goes so far as to state that, in the long history of man, "it is doubtful whether such a critical food situation has ever been so worldwide." "We are grappling," says India's health and family-planning minister, "with the most serious problem any nation has ever had to deal with"—impending starvation.

Girdling the globe at its equatorial bulge is a belt of hunger. Above it live the 1.4 billion inhabitants of the northern developed nations, whose advanced industry and agriculture permit them the luxury of worrying about reducing diets instead of diet deficiencies. Below it are the potentially prosperous lands of the southern hemisphere's temperate zone. The only exportable food surplusses now left in the world are produced by the highly capitalized agricultures of the larger industrialized countries, including Australia, Argentina, Canada, and the United States, which have in recent years produced twice their own domestic food requirements. Europe and China produce about as much food as they consume.

Most of the 2.5 billion citizens of the underdeveloped world live in the equatorial belt. *Time* states that nearly all of them are ill-fed, at least sixty percent are malnourished, and twenty percent more are starving. Today, famine is rampant in Bangladesh, Ethiopia, the African nations of the Sahel (Chad, Mali, Mauritania, Niger, Senegal, and Upper Volta), Gambia, and areas of Tanzania and Kenya. Near-famine also plagues parts of northern Nigeria as well as Bolivia, Syria, and Yemen. One poor harvest could bring massive hunger to India, the Sudan, Guyana, Somalia, Guinea, and Zaire; Angola, with its wars, verges on starvation. In a score of other countries the populace faces chronic food shortages: among them are Indonesia, the Philippines, and Haiti.

The Soviet Union does not at this time face mass famine. But in the mid-eighties it has a more critical food situation than it has faced previously in this half of the century. Its projected grain-crop expectations of 215.7 million tons for a year recently turned out to be a 137 million-ton crop—78.7 million tons short of its needs. *U.S. News and World Report* notes that "for the first time in years, ordinary Russians are talking about possible food shortages. . . . This year's disastrous grain harvest is reducing bread supplies [and] there are reports of rationing." The leader of the Soviet Union Mikhail Gorbachev was minister of agriculture from 1978-1984. During every one of those years, far less grain was grown than would meet domestic needs. Every harvest was classified a crop failure.

Several critical areas of possible solution need to be looked at. There is, of course, the matter of overpopulation. Noted Isaac Asimov at the U.N.-sponsored International Conference on Population in Mexico City: "Population growth at current rates will create a world without hope, gripped by starvation and desperation. It will be worse than a jungle, because we have weapons immensely more destructive and vicious than teeth and claws." The Secretary-General of the United Nations reckons man's greatest despair is "the unprecedented growth of the world's population." Approximately one-quarter of all the people who have ever lived are alive today. The human race numbered a half-billion when Jesus was on earth, a billion a century ago, two billion in 1920, five billion today, and at its present rate of increase will double to ten billion in a single generation. (The McWhirter brothers of London, authors of *The Guinness Book of World Records,* have calculated that, given the present geometric rate of human population increase, there would be one person for every square yard on earth by A.D. 2500; by A.D. 3700, humanity would outweigh the earth itself; and by A.D. 7975, there would be enough bodies to fill all space in the known universe.)

What is so grave is that, according to United Nations projections, eighty-five percent of the increase of the world's population in the remainder of this century will be in the underdeveloped countries, where, on the average, populations will double in thirty years if they continue at their present three percent-per-year rate of increase. What is of grave concern is that the underdeveloped countries with their tremendous growth in populations are on a collision course with starvation.

Birth control—that's the answer, say many in the Western world. Not so, say Pope John Paul II and the official Catholic church worldwide. Artificial birth control, warns the pope, is fraught with "serious consequences," and he assures the world that the stand of the Catholic church will not change. As 130 countries send delegates to the United Nations World Population Conference, the American delegation warns that failure to universalize artificial birth control will imperil the world of the future. The Soviet Union and China countered that the West's concern to impose artificial birth control was part of an "imperialistic" myth aimed at keeping the developing countries in subjugation. The underdeveloped nations have generally resisted birth control as an answer to their problems. They insist instead that "industrial nations should share their wealth with poor countries in a new economic framework." This was a rather blunt reply to such committed advocates of artificial birth control as Senior Editor Marshall Loeb of *Time*, who editorializes that a look at the jarring mathematics of starvation reveals that "the crisis will get worse until we in the West demand that the underdeveloped countries decrease their population growth."

But will these demands be effective? Objectively, after years of trying to sell birth control promotions to the underdeveloped countries, Dr. Justin Blackwelder of the Environmental Fund in Washington, D.C., concedes, "Birth control simply isn't working. Couples in most impoverished countries want a large number of children because many will die. Children, you see, are the parents' only security in their old age." And so the populations of the underdeveloped countries are soaring.

And what have the skyrocketing price increases of the last few years done to the food production potential of the underdeveloped countries? The *South China Morning Post* carries an article on "Food, Fuel, and Fertilizer," in which a Chinese writer argues very closely and rationally that the trebling of wheat prices was not nearly as serious a blow to the underdeveloped countries as the quadrupling of oil prices, because agricultural equipment runs on oil. Most serious of all, insofar as food production was concerned, was the trebling of the price of commercial fertilizers, an increase that occurred because ninety-three percent of the fertilizers of the world are petrochemically based.

Just what relationship does this grave biological prospect of proliferating human famine have on the matter of World War III and the coming again of Jesus Christ? Dean Rusk told a gathering of 4,000 educators that the problem of starvation was one which, if not solved, would bring on a war out of sheer human desperation. Man can expect "wars as nations struggle for territory to accommodate population pressures," editorializes the *Philadelphia Inquirer*. According to *Time*, key leaders today have many "fears that radical poor nations" will coerce more productive nations into "giving up their wealth by threatening a nuclear holocaust." Tanzania's Julius Nyerere, speaking for the Group of 77, a consortium of developing countries within the United Nations, said to the Commonwealth Society in London recently, "It is not right that the vast majority of the world's people should be forced into the position of beggars without dignity. We demand change, and the only question is whether it comes by dialogue or confrontation." Is this one more milestone along the road to World War III?

Finally, let it be said that there is One who is concerned about housing and feeding the world. It is Jesus! *Time* asks if there is really anyone who cares that a third of mankind lives in near hopeless despair. There they are, in every part of the world. "Whether they are called favelas, ranchos, bustees, barriadas, or bidonuilles, there is a tragic sameness about these hovels where millions live and die: the fragile shacks made of cardboard or rusting corrugated sheet metal, the famished children's distended bellies, the inescapable stench of human beings packed tightly together without ready access to water or toilets." Will Jesus allow the social situation of the world to deteriorate much longer? Because He is God, and God is good, He's got to come back soon.

Extraordinarily significant was a recent gathering—significant because of its sponsor. Held in Montreal, and drawing distinguished delegates from throughout the world, the Right to Food Conference was sponsored by the associates of Ben-Gurion University of the Negev, Israel. After reviewing the depressing statistics of how the world is moving toward polarized feast and famine, toward prosperity and poverty, they resolved that there is plenty of food in the world, and potential for much more. But the problem is "political": the present systems of government unable—or unwilling—to distribute the food and housing available to the billions who are in critical need. They agonized, quoting Maynard Keynes, that "in the long run we're all dead" unless we have "the millennium or the revolution" (*Toronto Star*, June 3, 1984). In fact, "the millennium" is what will provide peace and plenty throughout the world. And what was so very significant about the Right to Food Conference was that it is sponsored by Israel. One day, the ancient prophets assured, Jerusalem will be the Millennial Capital of the world. Prophesied Isaiah, "Jerusalem . . . in the last days . . . shall be exalted . . . and all nations shall flow unto it. . . . for out of Zion shall go forth the law; and the word of the Lord from Jerusalem. . . . [God] shall judge [all] nations, . . . and they shall beat their swords into plowshares" (2:1-4).

Certainly Christians are to be in the vanguard of social compassion. Read again Jesus' Sermon on the Mount. Read again of His pronouncements at the judgment as recorded in Matthew 25. Read again about Christ's feeding the five thousand—and the four thousand. May we, His disciples, keep telling that story, and let us not forget that all four evangelists recorded the feeding of the five thousand—the only miracle recorded in all four Gospels. This compassion is a part of the Gospel of Jesus Christ. The ultimate gospel message, however, is that Jesus Christ is coming again to set up His kingdom of peace and plenty.

Meanwhile, as Billy Graham said to the 2,500 delegates at the Religious Broadcasters Convention in Washington, "I do not believe in unilateral disarmament. But how can we be indifferent to the millions and millions who live on the brink of starvation each year, while the nations of the world spend a trillion dollars each year on weapons?"

Another signal of His coming again which will cause enormous social upheaval, Jesus assured, would be "earthquakes in various places" (Matthew 24:7). *Time* tells us that there have been as many massively destructive earthquakes in the past twenty-five years as there were in the previous two hundred. And there have been as many deaths in earthquakes in the last ten years—well over a million—as there were in the last hundred. There were the Algerian and Italian earthquakes of 1980 which wiped out an estimated 23,000 lives; two years later an earthquake on the same Arabian peninsula where Israel is located killed a thousand in Yemen.

During a recent year, there was a series of serious earthquakes over the course of six months. First Guatemala suffered an earthquake which was North America's greatest killer disaster ever—22,000 lives were lost and a million left homeless.

Grief, starvation, and disease prevailed in the 2,700 square miles of the quake zone. Three months later, a quake killing a thousand people rocked northern Italy, Yugoslavia, Austria, West Germany, Czechoslovakia, and Belgium; another, eight times as powerful, struck in southern Russia; within a few days of this a comparable quake hit China near the Burmese border. (Neither Russia nor China disclosed the number of casualties.) An earthquake next hit the Vancouver area (the most severe earthquake there in fifty-four years), soon followed by a coast-to-coast earthquake which rocked across Mexico. Within days, Peru was in the throes of another series of convulsive earthquakes, a grim reminder of the 66,794 who had lost their lives in 1970 in what has been called the largest natural disaster in the history of the modern Americas. Then Indonesia was victimized by an earthquake that killed an estimated 9,000 people; this was followed by one in the Philippines, where some 8,000 lost their lives.

It was during that six-month period that perhaps the worst killer earthquake in history struck the Greater Peking area, decimating the population of Tangshan. A report in the *Ming Pao* newspaper reckoned 900,000 dead. The *Hong Kong View*, with full reports in, estimated the dead at one million. The *View* pointed out that the Chinese word for earthquake is *tien-fan-ti-fu*, meaning "heaven tumbles, earth cracks," and warned that such a strong earthquake meant the fall of a dynasty. In four weeks Mao Tse-tung was dead. The Chinese tradition that God in heaven always has the last word was not dead. Mao Tse-tung, while he lived, was worshipped by more people than any more person ever. Mao called himself creator, redeemer, savior. A billion living and dead Chinese called him messiah, lord, everlasting sun. "My glory will I not give to another," warned God. I the Lord of Hosts will come with . . . earthquake (Isaiah 42:8, 29:6). In the book of Revelation we read of judgmental earthquakes yet to come. For example, in Revelation 11:13 we read that "at that very hour there was a severe earthquake and a tenth of the city collapsed" (NIV).

Earthquakes are on the increase everywhere. It is an inexorable law of nature. Seismologist Gabriel Lablanc declared that "once there has been an earthquake in an area we know it will experience more earthquakes and they will be of equal or greater magnitude. A case in point is Colorado, where until

1962 there was not a solitary measurable earthquake, according to the *New York Times*. Since then, over 3,000 earthquakes have been registered.

As accurate a history of earthquakes as seismologists are able to assemble indicates that there were 137 "major" earthquakes in the fourteenth century; 174 in the fifteenth; 253 in the sixteenth, and so on up through this century, in which we have already had 2,250 "major" earthquakes. This works out, in terms of major earthquakes, to an increase of 2,189 percent in six centuries. "Forecast: EARTHQUAKE," the title of a *Time* cover story, gives a comprehensive account of how geophysicists from around the world are currently warning that, in any of the high number of densely populated areas on the planet, a million or more people could be wiped out in a cataclysmic earthquake, virtually without warning.

So then, both from the predictions of scientists and from the prophecies of the Bible, the future, insofar as earthquake destruction is concerned, looks bleak. Perhaps the most quoted seismologist in the world today is Dr. Don Anderson, director of the Cal Tech Seismology Laboratory, Pasadena. To the American Association for the Advancement of Science, Dr. Anderson warns of concrete "evidence the earth may soon suffer a number of cataclysmic earthquakes." He points out that "major earthquakes occur when the earth's daily rotation slows, and when the North Pole wobbles away from its normal position with respect to the heavens." Anderson goes on: "The earth's rotation has been slowing at about one-thousandth of a second daily for five years. And the North Pole has been wobbling as much as 15 feet out of normal position." The conditions are ripening for "major disastrous earthquakes"—worldwide. When you add to this the fact that when the thirty-nation Disarmament Conference met in Geneva it was confirmed that it is now "conceivable in certain areas to provoke an earthquake or gigantic tidal wave," you reach the realization that the times are ripe for earthquakes to inflict destruction such as the world has never seen.

As we turn to the Revelation and read what is ahead, let us keep in mind that the Middle East is one of the most earthquake-prone areas of the world. The recent earthquake in Turkey that killed 3,000 took place where the seven churches of the Revelation had been located. Let us also keep in mind that Jesus said the Middle East is going to be the stage of "great tribulation, such as was not since the beginning of the world to this time, no, nor ever shall be" (Matthew 24:21 KJV). It will be a time when people will "flee to the mountains" (v.16). When an earthquake hits, people inevitably do two things: they run for cover, and they call out to God—in curses or in prayer. In a Palm Springs (California) high school hangs a sign which reads: "In the event of an earthquake, the Supreme Court ruling against prayers in school will be temporarily suspended."

Ed McMahon, co-host on Johnny Carson's "Tonight Show," assures whoever will listen that experiencing an earthquake "in fact" differs sharply from experiencing one in pretense, as in *Earthquake* or *The City That Waits to Die*. "Anyone around Los Angeles that day will never forget February 9, 1971," noted McMahon. "I was hitting the sack about 4:00 a.m. An hour and fifty-nine minutes later, all hell broke loose. My first reaction was that some unseen force was trying to break down the walls of my room. . . . I was on the seventeenth floor and was positive our building was going to pitch too far and crash to the ground. I have had a couple of close calls flying in two wars, but I have never been more frightened than that morning. How do I feel about living on a shelf that is moving in the opposite direction from the shelf beneath it? When those two shelves grinding against each other have had it, maybe so have I," McMahon reflects. In fact, Mr. McMahon, the whole of mankind should be reminded every time they read of, let alone experience, "earthquakes," that Jesus Christ is coming again and the end of the age is approaching. An earthquake is one of His means to call us to repentance, as it was with the Philippian jailer (Acts 16:16-40).

I was in England with Billy Graham when the severest earthquake to strike Britain in precisely a century hit. We were in Liverpool, just a few miles from the epicenter. Replying to the *Liverpool Echo* (July 19, 1984), many people on the street, terror-stricken, reacted, "It has to have something to do with the Billy Graham meetings." The consummation of the age and the descent of the Son of God with His saints to reign throughout the world, bringing harmony out of chaos and beauty out of ashes, is recorded in Zechariah and Revelation. In other words, disaster will precede the coming of Christ. Certain seismologists are warning of such a disaster in the Middle East, with Africa and Europe pushing at each other from beneath and Europe being shoved eastward and the Middle East westward. In Revelation 16:18-21, we read, "Then there came flashes of lightning, rumblings, peals of thunder and a severe earthquake. No earthquake like it has ever occurred since man has been on earth. So tremendous was the quake the great city split into three parts, and the cities of the nations collapsed. . . . Every island fled away and the mountains could not be found. From the sky huge hailstones of about a hundred pounds each fell upon men. And they cursed God on account of the plague of hail, because the plague was so terrible." It could be conjectured that God will simply allow natural laws in His universe to cause the polar ices to break up and storm over the continents in a cataclysmic blizzard; or it could be a shooting of water, say, eight or nine miles into the air where the temperature is minus forty degrees and the water freezes into ice balls. Who knows what God has in mind? It is my belief that this greatest earthquake in the history of man on the earth will be the cataclysmic leveler that plows and harrows the topography of Planet Earth at the time of Armageddon and prepares the mountainous and desert areas of the world for the lush worldwide "paradise restored" that it will be during the Millennium.

Chapter Four

Philosophy and
the Coming Christ

In the wake of the proliferation of the atomic bomb Albert Einstein brooded that nuclear know-how has changed everything except the way men think. Our thinking, when God is left out, becomes more of an adversary than an advocate! Asks Ivy League pundit Mary McGrory plaintively, "Have you ever seen so many thinkers openly agonizing over 'the end of the world'?" Jonathan Schell, in his *The Fate of the Earth* (called by many recent philosophers a "new Bible"), warns that if the "unthinkable" becomes "thinkable" than "you will be dead, and you, and you—all of you reading this will be dead, and your children, and your grandchildren and their grandchildren to infinity. And no one will ever dig down through the layers of death to find the ruin of this holy citadel we inhabit today. There is no one to dig." Writes philosopher/physician Lewis Thomas in his new book, *The Unforgettable Fire*, "The whole earth is being set up as an altar for a burnt offering, a monstrous human sacrifice to an imagined god with averted eyes."

"Thinking the unthinkable" is the expression the late Herman Kahn coined to describe the actual advent of nuclear war. And think we must. When our Canadian prime minister remarked on national television that "most of our problems are in our minds," he was simply reflecting the maxim of the ancient Solomon who reasoned that "as a man thinketh . . . so is he" (Proverbs 23:7). We are not always what we think we are. But what we think: we are! Thinking does not always get us out of binds—very often it gets us into one. That is where man is today.

Francis Bacon, who once argued that "all good moral philosophy is but the handmaid to religion," also cautioned that "a little philosophy inclineth man's mind to atheism; but depth in philosophy bringeth men's minds about to religion." St. Paul, himself a great philosopher and completely at home reasoning the Gospel with philosophers—as he did with the Athenian Stoics and Epicureans—exhorted the Colossians to "see to it that no one makes a prey of you by philosophy and empty deceit, according to human tradition" (Colossians 2:8 RSV); rather, "Set your minds on things that are above, not on things that are on earth," for "when Christ who is our life appears, then you also will appear with him in glory" (Colossians 3:2,4 RSV). In actuality, anticipation of Christ's coming again is the best intellectual stimulant that a people can have, not mere mental activity, but positive thinking. It imparts hope.

The most widely read philosophers of our time are not optimists. Currently, the most popular living American philosopher is Christopher Lasch. In his *Narcissism in an Age of Diminishing Expectations*, he surveys man philosophically as "plagued by depression, vague discontents, a sense of inner emptiness," and so crippled intellectually that he is capable of achieving "neither individual self-aggrandizement nor spiritual transcendence." Of the mood in academe, Michael Allen of Yale has said, "Students have fallen into terrible despair . . . so they're giving up . . . defeated, humiliated, and looking for a hiding place." Hungarian-Canadian psychiatrist Dr. Frank Somers, a widely quoted researcher, laments that seventy-five percent of the young expect to be nuked—perhaps within ten years.

Here is why the return of Christ is such good news. During a crusade which I was conducting on the West Coast, I was asked by Professor Lloyd Hayes, vice-president of the American Association of Philosophers, West, to speak and answer questions in three of his philosophy classes. In two of them, although I recollect having made no reference to the second advent of our Lord, students spontaneously asked, "Do you believe that Jesus Christ is coming again?" There was obviously real excitement in these questions. It is our only philosophic hope.

Jesus forecast that there would be striking resemblances between men in Noah's time and those who lived just prior to His return. One which is relevant here is that in the antediluvian era there were giants in the earth and the earth was filled with violence. They were intellectual giants to have advanced as rapidly as they did, yet violence overwhelmed them. The Oxford philosopher Trevor Roper reckons that man has undergone "a turning point," ushering in a "new age of violence, in which the whole world has capitulated to "a new character: a character of international anarchy." Bemoans Prime Minister Margaret Thatcher in the *London Times*: "We are reaping what was sown in the sixties, the fashionable theories of permissive clap-trap! . . . Our children are fed on a daily diet of violence unparalleled in our history. That diet can numb the sense of shock and render acceptable those things which we should reject." Scientists are telling us that the survival of civilization is being threatened by thermonuclear annihilation. Philosophers say anarchy will overturn us, if bombs do not get to us first.

The philosophers of the past have tended to be theists. Today—while scientists tend more and more to believe in God—the philosophers who are most studied are, in intellectual posture, atheists. Immanual Kant never attempted *a posteriori* to prove the existence of God, but believed in the necessity of believing in Him *a priori*. It was a subjective essential for man to believe in God. Regarding eternal life, Kant argued for immortality on the basis of heaven being necessary for the believer to develop fully his moral faculties. Schleiermacher, Hegel, Ritschl, Dostoevsky, and Kierkegaard (the father of modern existentialism) were all devout believers in God. But some of their successors—such as Jean-Paul Sartre, Albert Camus, Julian Huxley, Bertrand Russell, Karl Jaspers, and Martin Heidegger—have felt it preferable to write from an atheistic stance. After all, their mentors, Darwin, Freud, and Marx, were atheists who have enormously influenced twentieth-century life along the whole spectrum of modern thought, social engineering and conduct.

St. Jude portended men "denying the only Lord God" (Jude 4). This would condition one-time Christian nations for the coming Antichrist who shall "speak great words against the most High" (Daniel 7:25); nor will he "regard the God of his fathers" (Daniel 11:37). It is he who, according to St. Paul, "opposeth and exalteth himself above all that is called God" (2 Thessalonians 2:4).

Never before has a monolithic political system been superstructured on the foundation of atheism as has international communism. Karl Marx insisted in his *Communist Manifesto* that his system could only operate on an atheistic base, and his thesis has been undeviatingly adhered to by Marxists throughout the world. Nobel Prize-winning novelist Alexander Solzhenitsyn was unable to have the word "God" printed in capitalized form in the Soviet Union. The pattern Marxists have adopted is not immediately to uproot and exterminate the Church, but to wait until the time is propitious. It was only recently that Albania claimed to become "the first atheist state in the world"; its *Nendori* reported that 2,169 churches, monasteries, etc., had been closed and their adherents prevented from even minimal expressions of religion. As St. Paul forebode, "They have bartered away the true God for a false one, and have offered reverence and worship to created things instead of to the Creator, who is blessed forever; amen" (Romans 1:25 NEB).

What is perhaps much more alarming is the blatant atheism of university people in Western countries today. In the early 1980s, when I last held meetings at Oxford University, my alma mater, I noticed a radical change from the atmosphere five years before. The Humanist Group, which militantly opposes religion in general and Christianity in particular, had grown during that time from a membership of fifty-two to over a thousand, which was more than all the religious societies combined. Their graduates infiltrate the key communications and political posts. The late Julian Huxley arrogated: "God is no longer a useful hypothesis. A faint trace of God still broods over the world like the smile of a Cheshire cat, but psychological science will rub even that form from the universe."

Many feel that the atheism which is rampant today is getting an assist, rather than a rebuttal, from the Church. In March 1985, the Right Reverend Douglas Feaver retired as the longtime bishop of Peterborough. His comments with regard to his fellows in the House of Bishops was revealing: "They'd believe anything, provided it's not in the Holy Scripture." The pope laments the horizontalization of religion, which turns the

Church into a social convenience rather than a spiritual force. God has been more and more depersonalized by theologians, who too often refer to Him merely as "the ground of being," "the force of life," "the principle of love," or "ultimate reality." This creates the impression of divesting Him of the capacity to be experienced and to establish and maintain a personal relationship with His children through faith in Jesus Christ as Savior and Lord. James McCord, president of Princeton Theological Seminary, lamented that "today, we are at the end of a theological era, with the old theological systems a shambles." Senator Frank Carlson grieves that increasing numbers of North Americans have lost "all sense of the sacred, the moral, and the ethical. But the spiritual leaders from both the laity and the priesthood are often found in the forefront of this irreligious retreat from sacred things. The criticisms of God rank well above almost all other criticisms of the hour. More people—in more ways and on more occasions—cast doubt, hurl darts, and throw charges against God such as this society has never seen in all of its history."

From Germany comes a Lutheran church booklet, *Mit Einander für Einander Beten,* which deplores the fact that "the majority of our people are members of the Church, and are really unbelievers." A perusal of the widely publicized Gallup Poll on religious beliefs of Europeans and North Americans reveals that an astonishing percentage of actual church members are atheists. That's like a child living at home who doesn't believe in mother.

Atheism as a philosophy of life is not content today to go its own way. Its proponents are getting more and more egotistical, haughty, militant, and aggressively scornful of believers. This philosophic stance, the Scriptures teach, is indicative of the need for, and fact of, Christ's return. "Note this first," anticipated St. Peter, "in the last days there will come men who scoff at religion and live self-indulgent lives" (2 Peter 3:3 NEB). "You must remember, beloved, the predictions of the apostles of our Lord Jesus Christ," St. Jude forewarned, " 'in the last time there will be scoffers, following their own ungodly passions' " (Jude 17,18 RSV). In the last days, presaged St. Paul, men will be "heady, high-minded, swollen with conceit." We have now reached a point in time, unique in history, lamented

Pedro Arrupe of the Jesuits, when the world is in the grip of a completely "godless society."

A glance at activities and student newspapers at universities and colleges reveals how the popular trend today is to hold the Church in derision. Essays, plays, and novels constantly use Christ's name in profanity. The national news media carry accounts of how Jesus Christ was burned in effigy on the campus of a college whose pioneering president was America's greatest nineteenth-century revivalist. Student activists in California form a denomination of devil-worshipers, leaders of which are "Satan's Ministers," who put on "devil's horns" and conduct services, including nationally televised wedding ceremonies.

In Canada, when Madalyn Murray O'Hair, the American crusader for atheism as an official establishment, faced the nation in a popular television program, thousands of students in one of the universities gave her repeated standing ovations; whereas, when a clergyman was on, a few weeks later, they jeered. Why? Because "the carnal mind is at enmity against God" (Romans 8:7).

"Without God and without hope," philosophy must have a god. So into the vacuum steps Satan, "transformed into an angel of light." When I was a rather sensitive undergraduate, mentioning the "devil" or "Satan" would incur derision and invite a reputation for gross naiveté or unmitigated imbecility. Today the devil is openly doing a land-office business among youth, particularly on university campuses. "Satan-Worshipers" are no joke. They are serious-minded, militantly on the march, and captivating a cross section of the world's youth. Whole- and half-page newspaper write-ups, entire television programs, and leading magazine articles are devoted to propagating the movement. "The Process" (as their movement is sometimes known) is sharply on the increase. In one small city alone, 450 "ministers of Satan" were ordained. In Chicago, 4,000 gathered "to worship Satan." In England, the movement is so strong that a member of parliament claims seventy-eight percent of secondary students have been in touch with a wizard or witch. According to the *Los Angeles Times,* whole villages in Russia are under the domination of wizards and witches. Voodoo is now as prevalent in Brazil as in Zimbabwe. The movement is veritably "worldwide." Dungeons and Dragons, a game which originated on a university campus and is becoming an obsession of students in the 1980s, is inarguably based on devil-worship. It has been blamed in courts of law across North America for a host of suicides and murders. It is also rather ironic that Arthur Lyons, the chronicler of the Satan movement, entitles his best seller *The Second Coming: Satanism in America*. The author, a familiar figure on late-night talk shows, makes the point: "The monster slouches toward Bethlehem to be born."

Is this satanic atheism, this ribald scoffing, getting our generation anywhere? Dr. Irwin Moon reckons that more new facts are discovered by man today in 24 hours than in 2,000 years of ancient history. Yet, according to *Time*, in a cover story on contemporary philosophy, all is confusion, doubt, all issues a vague and sickly gray. St. Paul prophesied that, in the last days, people will be "always learning and yet never able to grasp the truth" (2 Timothy 3:7, Phillips). Why? Because they "defy the truth; they have lost the power to reason, and they cannot pass the tests of faith" (2 Timothy 3:8 NEB). No commentary could more accurately describe our generation of jaded intellectualism, mired in the quicksands of sophisticated vagary. Of Sigmund Freud's original cloister of twelve psychiatrists, seven committed suicide, saying to the world that the avant-garde ideas of the twentieth century simply did not bring fulfillment. The Schizophrenia Foundation of Psychiatrists in the United States now reveals that psychiatrists, who are supposed to have the answers for the problems of our generation, commit suicide at the rate of six times that of the general public. The times are "out of joint," as Shakespeare would say.

The American sociologist Dr. Kay Jeffrey has demonstrated beyond all doubt that education escalates crime if it is not accompanied by some moral or spiritual elevator. For the last several years of his life, the most-read philosopher of his time, French existentialist Jean-Paul Sartre, was in a tangle with the French government over lawless attitudes and actions. Albert Camus philosophically explained this intellectual malaise in his *Revolt*. It is no longer a matter of the slave against his master or the poor against the rich, but of a man against creation. It is a metaphysical revolt. Man is in a continual state of tension:

nothing has either rhyme or reason and evil and virtue seem mere chance and caprice. This is illustrated in Philip Roth's best seller, *Portnoy's Complaint*, in which Roth's character, although well aware of his ethnic, sociological and Freudian hang-ups, is still racked by guilt and tension—"torn by desires, that are repugnant to my desires."

The sequel to this is that man is not only pragmatically but also philosophically dishonest. "His word is his bond" can no longer often be said. St. Paul predicted that in "the last days" men would be "truce-breakers" and "traitors." So morally irresponsible is the human race becoming that Konrad Lorenz, the writer on thermonuclear warfare, reckons that if there is a missing link, it is more likely to be the one between plants and animals than between animals and humans, for man has, beneath his surface, a beastly nature which could trip the nuclear trigger to annihilate a whole section of humanity.

In F. H. Underhill's *In Search of Canadian Liberalism,* the author points out that philosophically the modern wave of liberalism which swept over the Western world is "in essence a Utopian faith" based on the innate goodness of "human nature." Modern psychologists have now, however, uncovered "deep subconscious instinctive drives in us which pervert our reason." We have been rudely awakened to the fact of our "original sin" which has issued in "outbursts of the demonic elements in human nature whose existence we had forgotten. We have learned to our horror the terrible potentialities of man's inhumanity to man."

Another philosophical sign that Jesus Christ is coming again is that our generation is replete with peace pretenders. Forecast St. Paul to the Thessalonians, "As far as times and seasons go, my brothers, you don't need written instructions. You are well aware that the day of the Lord will come as unexpectedly as a burglary to a householder. When men are saying, 'Peace and security,' catastrophe will sweep down upon them as suddenly and inescapably as birth pangs to a pregnant woman" (1 Thessalonians 5:1-3, Phillips). Jeremiah warned of those who say, "Peace, peace; when there is no peace" (Jeremiah 6:14). Let the record be kept straight. We are to strive for peace and pray for peace. "If possible, so far as it lies with you, live at peace with all men" (Romans 12:18 NEB), exhorted St. Paul;

and one of Jesus' beatitudes was "Blessed are the peacemakers." Indeed, St. Peter admonished believers that they "look forward to new heavens and a new earth, the home of justice. With this to look forward to, do your utmost to be found at peace" (2 Peter 3:13,14 NEB). There is no want for peace pinings in our world today. Two thousand books have been written on the theme of peace since World War II. A Jewish rabbi writes on *Peace of Mind*, a Catholic bishop on *Peace of Soul,* and Billy Graham on *Peace With God* (re-issued in 1985 by Word).

However, peace pretenders wholesaling peace propaganda populate our world today. According to the *Vancouver Province,* there are thirty-six front organizations for Marxism, every one of which includes the word "peace." (Sometimes one watches televised goings-on in the United Nations and hears more ignited notions than he sees united nations.)

H.F. Armstrong, the longtime friend of presidents, published his *Peace and Counterpeace: From Wilson to Hitler* in which he describes how, when he met Hitler in the 1930s, Der Führer engaged in a sixty-minute, nonstop monologue in which he disclaimed any desire for war. He was, he ranted on and on, a "man of peace." As the world discovered, Hitler became the most monstrous warmonger in history. His "peace, peace" could have been translated "war, war." As the Psalmist said, "When they say peace, war is in their heart."

When Mikhail Gorbachev emerged as head of the Soviet Union in his initial address to the world, banner headlines signalled: SOVIET LEADER PREACHES PEACE. Prime Minister Mulroney, in Moscow for the funeral of Konstantin Chernenko, personally apprised Mr. Gorbachev that the whole country of Canada is praying for peace. But it probably fell to Margaret Thatcher to make the most balanced assessment: "I like Mr. Gorbachev. We can do business together." But Mrs. Thatcher continued that the West should be warned that in the closing years of the twentieth century "the goal of the Soviet Union remains 'the total triumph of socialism all over the world.' "

A few years ago, a declaration made a quarter of a century earlier by the secretary of the executive committee of the Comintern was read on the floor of the American Senate. Assured

the Russian leader, "War to the hilt between Communism and Capitalism is inevitable. Today, of course, we are not strong enough to attack. Our time will come in 20 or 30 years. To win, we shall need the element of surprise. The bourgeoisie will have to be put to sleep. So we shall begin by launching the most spectacular peace move on record. There will be electrifying overtures and unheard-of concessions. Capitalist countries, stupid and decadent, will rejoice to cooperate in their destruction. They will leap at another chance to be friends. As soon as their guard is down, we shall smash them with our clenched fists." "The object of Soviet Communism," asserted Stalin, "is 'victory of Communism throughout the world—by peace or war.' "
I would like to lapse into the sentimental dream of my secular contemporaries that all is well with the West and Communism today, but I am compelled by my reading of the Bible to say that this is simply not so. "Watch ye therefore!"

Of the Soviet military with their "all sorts of armour," the Word of God states plainly, "Thus saith the Lord God: Behold I am against thee!" (Ezekiel 38:4,3). That doesn't mean that Billy Graham should have any less zeal to reach the souls of people in the USSR than he has for those in the United States or the United Kingdom. Nor does it mean that we should have less enthusiasm for feeding the helpless starving bodies of Ethiopians than for the hungry in our inner cities (Ezekiel 38:5 prophesied that the Ethiopian regime would ally itself with the Russians; see *Globe and Mail,* Nov. 26 and Dec. 24, 1984, articles by Paul Fromm, research director of Citizens For Foreign Aid Reform). But neither does it mean that we should be duped by the peaceniks of the Communist world who keep saying, "Peace, peace," when they're planning for "sudden destruction." President Mitterand of France was so right when, amid the millions of peace marchers, he remarked, "The Communists have the missiles, and we have the marchers."

Other conditions contributing to spiritual decline and philosophical confusion today is the crowdedness of our planet and the anonymous nature of our mass culture. It is "a long twilight zone, year in and year out," as John Kennedy put it in his inauguration address. We are surrounded by milling millions who want anonymity, "a world that is more and more impersonal" (as a lead editorial in the *Toronto Star* noted). The

Revelation of Jesus Christ (an "apocalyptic vision . . . more real" today than it has been to "anyone since St. John on Patmos," as C.S. Lewis put it) foretold of how in the times of the Lord's return and those events leading up to it, there would be 10,000 times 10,000 here, an army of 200 million there, and a great number which no man could number in another place. Marshall McLuhan wrote that we were living in a "global village." A team of psychiatrists jointly write an article in a national weekly indicating that, as population pressure builds up, there is a concurrent buildup of animal ferocity in human disguise. Man is like a volcano about to erupt. Jamming the human race into a global ghetto will inevitably cause it to burst into a global conflagration.

Man has reacted to the encroachments and pressures of the current cauldron by striking out on a hedonistic pleasure binge, and the trend is bound to accelerate. Walter Reuther told Billy Graham that in twenty years it will be possible in a single year to produce one hundred times as much steel by one-hundredth the manpower. Peoples in the Western industrialized societies will work two days a week—perhaps less. The result of all this is surfeited pleasure-hunting, leading to "misery" and "wretchedness," signs of Christ's promised coming again. St. James spoke of the "last days" being a time when "rich men weep and howl for [their] miseries" (James 5:1), and that men would be insensitive to the fact that they were "wretched" and "miserable" despite the fact that they were "rich and increased in goods."

The American novelist John Barth expresses the philosophic dilemma of our times in the title of his novel: *Lost in the Funhouse*. People are trying to crowd into a funhouse full of joytoys to escape the stark realities of life, only to find themselves lost. Wrote the philosopher Bertrand Russell of himself, "I could think of nothing but suicide"; of the world around him he wrote, "Over man and all his works, night falls pitiless and dark." As James Russell Lowell despaired, "Life's emblem deep: a confused noise between two silences," so people everywhere are feeling.

Contemporary rock tells of the philosophic despair of many millions of teenagers. In my writings elsewhere, I quote from scores of current songs which express the absolute despair and inconsolable loneliness of our generation of youth; and it can do nothing but get worse. Lamented the late Fulton Sheen, "Our delinquent youths in America become delinquent because they have no missions, no purpose in life. Pour steam into a boiler and give it no work, and it will blow up. Youth is blowing up for the same reason."

The *Sunday Telegraph* in London was responsible, along with the Gallup International Poll, for the recent probing of the current state of mind of Europeans: "Religious beliefs are declining; morals also have slumped; honesty is on the wane; happiness is becoming increasingly hard to find; peace of mind is rare." The British Brains' Trust, appearing on BBC-TV, agreed unanimously that tragedy outlasts comedy because life is tragedy. And the *New York Times* opines that it seems that humor has nowhere near the place it once had in the American way of life.

Since God is love, it would not be right if Jesus Christ did not come back again and bring us into a state of philosophic fulfillment. The suicide rates of both North Americans and Europeans yield the facts that about eight times as many rich as poor, per capita; eight times as many highly educated as normally schooled, per capita; and eight times as many of those at the center of the "good-time" life as those at the drab fringes, commit suicide. Philosophically reduced to a formula, this reads that the more people earn, the more they learn; and the more they burn, the more they yearn for fulfillment. This throws all of our value molds back into the melting pot: especially when, according to Ann Landers' column, suicide would probably be in fourth place as a cause of death, if all the facts were known.

While this emptiness within is a characteristic of our times, the pressure from without is another sign that Jesus Christ is coming. Our Lord forecast that prior to His return there would be "distress of nations, with perplexity": that is, whole "nations will stand helpless, not knowing which way to turn," intimidated with "terror at the thought of all that is coming upon the world; for the celestial powers will be shaken. And then they will see the Son of Man coming on a cloud with great power and glory. When all this begins to happen, stand upright and hold your heads high, because your liberation is near" (Luke

21:25-28 NEB). These last two sentences make the philosophic posture of believers a most auspicious thing. But a world which is depending on any other hope than that afforded by Jesus Christ cannot be realistic and optimistic at the same time.

When an American secretary of defense committed suicide because of unendurable pressures, he reasoned, "This state of tension will continue for the rest of our lives, and those of our children." "We have to ask ourselves," brooded the late Walter Lippmann, "why do we find ourselves facing impossible choices wherever we turn?" Newspaper columns read: "Fatal Objections Were Found to Almost Every Decisive Step!"; "Cultivated Uncertainty Is the Order of the Day"; "Inexpressible Consternation!"; "Both Were Alike in Not Knowing Which Way to Turn or What to Do!"; "No Normalcy!" Philosopher C.E.M. Joad, formerly of Cambridge and famous for his appearances on the British Brains' Trust, reasoned, "You don't give your children dangerous toys until you know that they can handle them. But this is in fact what science has done." It has given man the wherewithal to exterminate himself at a time of tragically declining moral responsibility.

Tom Harpur described how Dr. Helen Caldicott, professor of medicine at Harvard and head of the 30,000-member Physicians for Social Responsibility, "electrified the delegates" who were gathered together in 1983 for the World Council of Churches in Vancouver as she depicted what would happen if nuclear weaponry is used. She lamented: "Ours is a terminally ill planet . . . the world's superpowers are like 9-year-old boys in a sandbox [only] they are building nuclear warheads, rather than sandcastles, and are setting the stage for a battle that could kill hundreds of millions of people in its first hour. . . . Millions more would die of radiation illness, starvation, uncontrolled epidemics and burns. Winds traveling hundreds of kilometers an hour would turn people into human missiles. All over the world, people would die of sunburn in less than 60 minutes. And subsequently, with loss of the protective atmosphere, 'another ice age could be induced by the cooling.' " Such rhetoric, month after month and year after year, ensures that on the universal psyche pressures worldwide are escalating. A TV program is entitled "Man Afraid." "The fact is that today the biggest single emotion which dominates our lives is fear," comments *U.S. News and World Report.* "I write this to frighten you," writes the Nobel Prize-winner Professor Urey, assuring us, "I am a frightened man myself. All the scientists I know are frightened—frightened for their lives—and frightened for your life."

In my travels to a hundred countries during my years as an evangelist, the secular organization I have most frequently addressed has been the Rotary International. I have spoken to tens of thousands of their worldwide membership of one million. When 15,000 of their leaders assembled in Toronto in June 1983, for the annual convention, there is hardly any argument that their numbers included many of the brightest and most responsible leaders on earth. Their addresses were, to a secular mind, depressing. In a major plenary session Dr. Bernard Lown, president of the International Physicians for the Prevention of Nuclear War warned ominously: "We are doomed. People must coerce their governments to stop this race to Armageddon." Dr. Lown, professor of cardiology at Harvard, noted that "a U.S. Senate committee reported there were 3,703 false alarms in the early warning system in an 18-month period—with 147 of them serious enough to require evaluation . . . four that 'nearly led to a nuclear exchange.' Human fallibility can play an even more important role . . . 115,000 U.S. military personnel have 'critical access' to nuclear weapons or their control." The problems seem, for man's future, insurmountable. One might add that Dr. Lown, being a Harvard professor of cardiology, was adding to the problems of his own profession by his honest appraisal, for Jesus warned that "hearts [would be] failing them for fear [of] those things which are coming on the earth."

Annihilation fears are not the only anxieties which build pressures that lead to heart failure. The *New York Times* explains: "Throughout the entire world, . . . issues that formerly took a century or more to come to a boil are in constant eruption. Everything is being bunched up—time, space, nations, peoples, issues. And everything has a fuse attached to it. The habits of nations, always variable, have become starkly irrational." Comments Kevin White, a mayor of Boston, "I think the most frustrating thing for new mayors is not being able to solve the problems of their cities. Many of them are quitting after one term these days." Dr. Roy Grinker of the Michael

Reese Hospital in Chicago comments on how these strains affect the heart and how the terrific pressures of the age we live in overload our coronary organs far beyond nature's provision. It was most necessary, then, that Jesus made His statements "Let not your heart be troubled" (John 14:1) and "Settle it therefore in your hearts" in connection with His return, so that His disciples might have fortification.

After reviewing the despairing facts of a world gone out of control, Paul Johnson of the elitist *New Statesman* in London concluded, "There are times when I feel that I would welcome an invasion from Mars." That, Mr. Johnson, is the way the whole world feels philosophically; however, it is not an invasion from Mars but rather the return of Jesus Christ which is the "desire of all people," whether or not they realize it—as the ancient prophet prognosticated. How can we solve our deep philosophic apprehensions? Robert Browning averred, "Shooting at fear with all the strength of hope." "We are saved by hope," affirmed St. Paul.

Why does the whole world not read the signs of the times and believe? *Intelligence Digest* of London, reviewing the plight of the times, reasons, "If not in present conditions, in what circumstances can people be roused?" As St. Peter projected, a sign of the coming of the Lord is that men would be "willingly ignorant"; and Jesus, in relating Dives' appeal from hell, declared that if men are impenitent, even one's rising from the dead to testify to the unseen world would not induce repentance.

Affirmed the great philosopher Immanuel Kant, "There is nothing good in the world or the universe which does not begin with the good will." The will is the hinge upon which the kingdom of God swings open. "If there be first a willing mind," St. Paul assured the Corinthians, "it is accepted according to that a man hath, and not according to that he hath not" (2 Corinthians 8:12). Henry Ward Beecher said there are only two classes of people in the world: the whosoever wills and the whosoever won'ts.

Man need not be ignorant of the way to heaven. In that passage on the return of Christ in 1 Thessalonians 4, which Cardinal Cushing recited at the funeral of President Kennedy, St. Paul urges, "I would not have you ignorant." He then defines

the basis of salvation and how we can go when Christ comes
again, "Believe that Jesus died and rose again, [for in this] we
have a definite message from the Lord." To those who accept
Jesus Christ as their Savior and Lord on this basis is the
assurance given: that they can surely know they will be His at
His coming, and forthwith forever.

Chapter Five

The Church and
the Coming Christ

On Christmas morning, 1984, Prince Charles leaned over to his eldest son, Prince William, heir to the British throne, and asked him where he was going that day. "To church," replied the two-and-a-half-year-old—to the obvious pleasure of his parents and the tens of millions who saw the scene on television.

Our Lord's first concern in this world is His Church, after all, "He loved it and gave Himself for it." Those of us who are its ministers should have that same love for the Church. Like Hermes, we exclaim, "The Church, this miracle of Earth." The Church has endured through twenty centuries, building up an immense body of goodwill born of 10,000 philanthropies; a network of missionary outposts unsurpassed by any organization in the world; an incomparable heritage of literature, art, and music; a long record of opposing tyranny; an ever-improving teaching apparatus; and, most importantly, the person and teachings of Jesus Christ.

There is no institution or organization on earth that can match the church for generous care for the world's starving and diseased. As one looks at the 1984-85 famine in twenty-two of Africa's fifty-two countries and asks who is giving the most sacrificially, it has certainly not been the Communist nations, who altogether gave about as much as the oil-wealthy Arab Moslem countries: which was virtually nil. Who did give generously? No group more generously than Christians! I serve as an elder at Peoples Church, which gave $300,000; and I was also a participant in David Mainse's 100 Huntley Telethon which raised $1,700,000 for the One-Hundred-Percent Africa Famine Fund. Fred Benson, a Baptist from Ontario, gave $400,000 from the sale of his farm, and this was only one of his many generosities. The American Council on Foundations revealed in 1985 that Christian churches collected $30 billion in 1984, 15 billion of which was given to the social needs of the poor—from the urban ghettos at home to the remotest outposts of the Third World. Notes the Council: through Christian "philanthropy, every conceivable need in society is being addressed," engaging with equal compassion in "redeeming souls [and] redeeming society" (*Toronto Star*, March 23, 1985).

Evangelicals, of course, believe in raising the resources apart from government taxation and management. This is the route that Prime Ministers Margaret Thatcher and Brian Mulroney, as well as President Reagan, prefer. Liberal churchmen, especially those with Marxist or socialist sympathies contend that philanthropy is a government function. Absorbing aggressive criticism from the left wing of British Anglicanism in 1985, Margaret Thatcher, with her conservative, evangelical roots, remonstrated: "There is a consistent tendency in our society to downgrade the creators of wealth, and nowhere is this attitude more marked than in the cloister (the church) and common room (academe). I make no complaint about that. After all, it wouldn't be spring, would it, without the voice of the occasional cuckoo."

The New Testament is clear. The primary task of the Church is to evangelize. I thought that one of the most satisfying witnesses to the world of how an individual finds God was affirmed by Her Majesty, Queen Elizabeth, in her annual Christmas address for 1984. Pointing to her small grandchildren in a very human family scene, she quoted from Jesus' words in Matthew 18:3, "Except ye be converted, and become as little children, ye shall not enter into the kingdom of heaven." The Queen herself gave her own life to Christ thirty years ago, led into the experience on a quiet Sunday afternoon by her guest at Buckingham Palace, Billy Graham.

However, it is currently inarguable that the Church has strayed far from its original commission. Dr. Verghese, an assistant secretary-general of the World Council of Churches, says that in the Church today there is a certain "form of godliness without the power thereof." It exists because we in the Church have too often tried to get people who have never committed their lives to Christ to act like Christians. Instead of reality, we have "form." According to the British author Leslie Steffard, the word "Christian" has become one of the vaguest words in the English language. "The church of today," says a leading psychologist, "is like an autumn leaf, dry and dead but retainings its form and structure."

Prior to His coming and the end of the age, Jesus cautioned His disciples that "the love of many shall wax cold" (Matthew 24:12). St. Paul described how in the last days, people would be "loving all the time what gives them pleasure instead of loving God" (2 Timothy 3:4, Phillips). Worshippers in whom love for God is replaced by love for pleasures are inevitably a people like those in the church in Laodicea, to whom our Lord said, "You are neither cold nor hot. I could wish that you were either cold or hot!" A chosen generation is too often a frozen generation today, too frequently as straight as a gun barrel, but just as empty. It is a bit at times like the moon, which radiates a light but gives off no heat; and even that light is occasionally darkness when the world comes between it and the sun. St. Peter, in his treatment of conditions as they would exist at the day of the Lord, spoke of "slackness." This loss of love, this reluctance to be either hot or cold, this slackness on the part of the Church, is all around us. Jude was writing at the conclusion of his letter to believers "in the last time": "But you, my friends, must fortify yourselves in your most sacred faith. Continue to pray in the power of the Holy Spirit. Keep yourselves in the love of God, and look forward to the day when our Lord Jesus Christ . . . will give eternal life" (Jude 20,21 NEB).

Much of the blame for this falling away from the Church must be placed on the unholiness of the Church itself, a condition which Jesus and His apostles clearly predicted would exist. Prior to His coming and the end of the age, Jesus said that "iniquity shall abound." "Imposters" in the Church, wrote St. Paul to Timothy, "will go on from bad to worse, deceivers and deceived" (2 Timothy 3:13 RSV). It is a painful thing to have to point out around us the fulfillments of these predictions. According to *Time*, one ecclesiastical body publishes a magazine which contains so much obscenity that it drives Roy and Dale

Rogers right out of their church. We pick up our papers and see where a prominent Episcopal bishop is unfrocked for chronic immorality, indecent sex suggestions, and habitual drunkenness.

With increasing frequency, every major denomination has its ranks depleted by this sort of thing. From Wisconsin comes the news that a play, *Paradise Now*, was staged in a church. During the performance nearly nude performers inspired the audience to strip; in fact, two females and two males did strip completely. What do we expect society at large to do when this kind of thing goes on in a church? In Ontario, a minister is exposed for not merely permitting but reportedly promoting premarital sex relations on the church premises. "In the final age," forewarned St. Jude, "there will be men who pour scorn on religion, and follow their own godless lusts." These men "split communities, for they are led by human emotions and never by the Spirit of God."

English Rector Stephan Hopkinson reckons that the Christian Church ought to set its approval upon homosexuality, not only on the part of the occupants of the pew, but also of those in the pulpit. While the United Church of Canada, like, say, the Anglican church, has an enormous number of conservative evangelicals among its clergy and membership, the mid-August General Assembly of 1984 was "overshadowed" by one dominating issue: whether or not to ordain self-confessed, practising homosexuals. Thank God, the vote was "No." But what cannot be let past was the "task force report: which says it cannot find any biblical [basis] to bar homosexuals" (*Toronto Star,* Aug. 13, 1984). C.H. Dodd, the liberal theologian at Mansfield, Oxford, where I did my D.Phil. research, was chairman of the New English Bible translation committee and insisted on rendering 1 Corinthians 6:9-14, "Sure you know that . . . no . . . homosexual [will] possess the Kingdom of God. Such were some of you. But you have been through the purifying . . . dedicated to God and justified through the Name of the Lord Jesus and the Spirit of our God [and at Christ's coming] He will raise us by His power."

In the churches of North America, there are now far too many radical departures from orthodoxy for these "gatherings" to legitimately be called churches. A Unitarian clergyman in Alberta gets national publicity by promoting in his "church" physical communion services, in which members are invited to come in bikinis and push together like shocks of sheaves until they feel the full emotional impact of physical fellowship. Anyone with normal responses knows the outcome of that kind of "communion." A council of churches commissions and pays for a film in which clergymen take off their clothes and face the congregation in the buff, and the naked body of an attractive young women is passed around from man to man as a form of "communion." Church members are being urged to move toward Sodom. St. Peter described how there shall be those who ". . . turn back and abandon the sacred commandments delivered to them! For them the proverb has proved true: 'The dog returns to its own vomit,' and, 'The sow after a wash rolls in the mud again' " (2 Peter 2:21,22 NEB).

Moral lapses and accidents have always occurred in the history of the Church, but this sort of thing being sponsored by churchmen is something previous generations simply could not have credited. "After 2,000 years of Christianity," bemoans the British peer Lord Halifax, the peoples of Christendom have "lapsed into degradation of the worst kind of paganism, as if men have no further use for Christianity."

What is conceivably worse than unholiness in the Church is hypocrisy. "God's Spirit specifically tells us that in later days," wrote St. Paul in his first letter to Timothy, "there will be . . . teachings given by men who are lying hypocrites" (1 Timothy 4:1,2, Phillips). Nothing is so ludicrous as to try and build a church from stumbling blocks. One of the most eloquent, if tragic, passages in the entire New Testament is where Jude is forecasting of those in the last time who would be "a menace to the good fellowship of your feasts, for they eat in your company without a qualm yet they care for no one but themselves. They are like clouds driven up by the wind, but they bring no rain. They are like trees with the leaves of autumn but without a single fruit—they are doubly dead, for they have no roots either. They are like raging waves of the sea producing only the spume of their own shameful deeds. They are like stars which follow no orbit, and their proper place is the everlasting blackness of the regions beyond the light" (Jude 12,13, Phillips). It is a most disastrous route to perdition which leads by way of the communion table.

Jesus, in that set of seven parables as recorded in Matthew 13, told two which left no mistake as to the exposure of hypocrites when He comes again. The one was of the wheat and the tares. The other parable states that "the kingdom of Heaven is like a net let down into the sea, where fish of every kind were caught in it. When it was full, it was dragged ashore. Then the men sat down and collected the good fish into pails and threw the worthless away. That is how it will be at the end of time. The angels will go forth, and they will separate the wicked from the good, and throw them into the blazing furnace, the place of wailing and grinding of teeth" (Matthew 13:47-50 NEB).

George Bernard Shaw was no friend of the Church. One of his really telling indictments against hypocrites was the sardonic statement that the trouble with Jesus Christ was that He had disciples. Why is the Church failing more and more to live up to its profession? According to biblical forecast, it is because of its departure from the historic faith. It is not because of its irrelevance, but because of its irreverence. "Now the Spirit speaketh expressly," wrote St. Paul to Timothy, "that in the latter times some shall depart from the faith, giving heed to seducing spirits" (1 Timothy 4:1). "Incapable of reaching a knowledge of the truth," Paul writes later, "these men defy the truth; they have lost the power to reason, and they cannot pass the tests of faith" (2 Timothy 3:7,8 NEB).

"A phenomenon of today's young candidates for the ministry," observes *Life,* "is that a great many of them do not have a positive acceptance that Jesus Christ is the Son of God." The late Bishop James Pike described in an internationally read magazine how he "jettisoned the trinity, the virgin birth and the resurrection." Surely this is just why he was "giving heed to seducing spirits," by involving himself on a national television network here in Canada in a séance.

In fact we need to be very much aware that "the Holy Spirit tells us clearly that in the last times," wrote the Apostle Paul, men will be "devil inspired" (1 Timothy 4:1 LB). During November 1984, I was asked to debate an eminent University of Toronto professor (who is in fact a clergyman) on prime time TV on our government-sponsored network. The question to be debated was: "Is there a Personal Devil?" That the thousands who phoned in their votes gave my side a seventy-five majority margin left me with mixed emotions. Actually I wish Satan didn't exist! He is a relentless adversary to our presentations of Christ. But that he does exist is dealt with 500 times in the Scriptures. Today sixty-seven percent of North Americans are convinced there is a devil and well they might be. As St. Peter wrote, "Your adversary the devil, as a roaring lion, walketh about, seeking whom he may devour" (1 Peter 5:8).

Yet St. Paul wrote of the devil, "Satan himself is transformed into an angel of light" (2 Corinthians 11:14). It seems today that reference to the devil is ubiquitous and casual. Currently, the most popular theatrical in Toronto is *The Devil's Wheel*, guaranteeing "edge of seat entertainment." Fay Weldon's *The Life and Loves of a She-Devil* is a best seller. A current list of movie titles includes: *Oh God, You Devil* (George Burns plays both); *Devil Girl From Mars*; and *The Devil-God*, which invites viewers to "enter the occult world and see the terror and shock or exorcism, witchcraft and necromancy."

But how do we best confront the devil in the world and the devil in the Church? By involving the Lordship of Jesus Christ. "For this purpose the Son of God was manifested, that he might destroy the works of the devil" (1 John 3:8). Many of us remember when the late Dr. Howard Clark, Anglican primate of Canada, addressed the Lambeth Conference of Bishops in London on one of the regrettable results of over-zealous ecumenism—the compromises we are making toward a rationalism which is secularizing our faith. "Is it any wonder," asked the primate, "that we have lost the power to communicate to the secular, unbelieving world the deep truths about God that are in our Christian tradition?"

Billy Sunday once remarked aptly that there wouldn't be so many non-going church members if there weren't so many non-going churches. The world expects the Church to have a message, a message it too often simply does not have. This is conspicuously true of too many of Canada's mainline churches. In Toronto, while the population of Metro increased twenty percent over a ten-year period, membership in the 152 churches of the Toronto Presbytery of the United Church of Canada dropped five percent. And what is much more a reason for pessimism, Sunday School enrollment declined by one-third.

Having written my doctor of philosophy thesis at Oxford

University twenty-five years ago on: "The Influence of North American Evangelism in Great Britain on the Origin and Emergence of the Ecumenical Movement During the Eighteenth and Nineteenth Centuries as Expressed in the Formation of the World Council of Churches in 1948," I took a particular interest in the Sixth Assembly of the World Council of Churches held in Vancouver in 1983. It is difficult to reconcile how liberal in theology and how far to the left politically and socially the W.C.C. pendulum has swung, with its origins and development having so totally evolved from the fiery revivalism, mass evangelism, and biblical evangelicalism of such giants of God as Jonathan Edwards, Charles G. Finney, Dwight L. Moody, and John R. Mott. The feature article in *Time* (Aug. 22, 1983) is headlined: "The Curious Politics of Ecumenism: To the World Council of Churches, the Soviets are Sinless." The ensuing commentary reads: "The World Council of Churches, an umbrella organization of 301 Protestant and Orthodox denominations with more than 400 million members, appears to be an ecclesiastical clone of the United Nations. [It] has seemingly evolved into a forum for relentless denunciations of the sins of . . . capitalism [while seeing a] 'no-evil' policy toward Communist regimes. [It affirmed] that Soviet troops should be allowed to stay in Afghanistan [and] recommended aid to the anti-Communist Afghan rebels be cut off. [It] also produced a harshly worded attack on U.S. Central American policy [praising] 'the life-affirming achievements' of the Nicaraguan government." Summed up *Time*, "This was vintage W.C.C. politics."

In an interview with *Maclean's* (Aug. 22, 1983), Dr. Robert Runcie, archbishop of Canterbury, conceded that much of what was affirmed was "only a dull echo of the liberal consensus." Prophesied St. Paul of "the last days": "The time will come when men will not put up with sound doctrine. Instead, to suit their own desires, they will gather around them a great number of teachers to say what their itching ears want to hear. They will turn their ears away from the truth and turn aside to myths" (2 Timothy 3:1; 4:3,4 NIV). Ross Irish writes in the *Toronto Star* (Aug. 17, 1983) that the W.C.C. seems to have no qualms about dispensing funds which end up financing weaponry used by guerrilla rebels to further communist revolution. Adds Darcy

Rector wryly, "It must irk the World Council of Churches to have to rely on the capitalist world for funding and for the religious freedom which is not found in non-capitalist societies . . . they know they can't get any money from communist or socialist countries. They are stuck with us, and we with them."

To the British novelist John Braine, the powerlessness of the Church lies in the fact that it "needs to make up its mind. Its trouble stems from the fact that nobody seems to know exactly what it stands for." When the Gospel is preached with authority, relevance, simplicity, and in its intrinsic purity, it will attract people, revolutionize them, and send them forth to live meaningful and directed lives. However, when it is diluted, vague, impersonal and smug, it is not fulfilling its mission. Here, too, is why the second advent is so little mentioned in its teaching. The reason for this neglect, according to C.S. Lewis, is that church members are so comfortable in this world that they cannot bring themselves to think about going to another. St. Peter concludes the third chapter of his second epistle in which he outlines the apocalyptic judgments of "the day of the Lord" with the appeal, "But you, my friends whom I love, are forewarned, and should therefore be very careful not to . . . lose your proper foothold" (2 Peter 3:17, Phillips).

Some of us recall vividly, when, back in the 1970s, the Anglican and United churches of Canada were contemplating a merger. They arranged contiguous national gatherings at Niagara Falls, the honeymoon capital of North America; and they presaged their merger with the publication of a new hymnal—one which attempts to edit out "obsolete" hymns and replace them with ones which would communicate to the young people of the final quarter of the twentieth century. Remarks by one clergyman to another were overheard by a newsman, "Strange isn't it, that we put in songs on the euphoria of the modern dance and the sacrament of sex, while removing such old timers as 'Amazing Grace.' With 'Amazing Grace' at the top of the charts this week, it seems to me that what we don't think will communicate to our youth, communicates to them very well!"

"I feel compelled," wrote St. Jude to saints (some of whom would live "in the last times"), "to make my letter to you an earnest appeal to put up a real fight for the faith which has been once for all committed to those who belong to Christ" (Jude 3, Phillips). This does not mean that we are to fight each other or discriminate against those who belong to other branches of the Christian church. It means "fight the good fight of faith," as St. Paul exhorted his protégé Timothy.

The apostle predicted that, as the end approached, many would be deliberately and even aggressively apostate, contriving to incite others to be hostile to the historic Christian faith. "First of all you must realize that in the last days mockers will undoubtedly come," wrote St. Peter in the last of his recorded chapters, "and they will say, 'What has happened to his promised coming? Since the first Christians fell asleep, everything remains exactly as it was since the beginning of creation!' They are deliberately shutting their eyes to a fact that they know very well" (2 Peter 3:3-5, Phillips). St. Paul, in the last of his recorded chapters carried the same concern: "I adjure you by his coming . . . the time will come when they will not stand wholesome teaching, but will follow their own fancy and gather a crowd of teachers to tickle their ears. They will stop their ears to the truth and turn to mythology" (2 Timothy 4:1,3 NEB).

In *A Gift of Prophecy*, Jeane Dixon was right to predict the infiltration of treason into the clergy of all denominations. One of the most remarkable conversions to Christ in the last few years was that of Malcolm Muggeridge. At the time of his conversion Muggeridge was editor of *Punch*, perhaps the world's foremost iconoclastic magazine—at least in English. Rector of the University of Edinburgh, he chose to give his initial testimony as occupant of that office, speaking to that distinguished body in the High Kirk of St. Giles. Actually his address was a "straightforward confession of faith" in Jesus Christ as Lord, entitled "Another King." In it he makes this astonishing statement, "As far as I am concerned, it is Christ or nothing." He added, "What I have just said is, I know, far more repellent to most of the present ecclesiastical establishment than any profession of skepticism or disbelief."

Just how little some churchmen are concerned to preserve or fend for the deity of Christ is evidenced in the fact that one American Episcopal bishop would like to scrap the Lambeth Conferences, the World Council of Churches, and the Roman

Catholic church in favor of a world religious organization which would put Buddha, Mohammed and any number of other sages and "prophets" on a par with Christ. Men have said things like this before, but they have not done so and retained office in any orthodox Christian denomination. I am personally acquainted with a famous English bishop who, despite Jesus' insistence on "You must be born again," requests, "Count me among the once born men." Pope John Paul II, in his Christmas address of 1984, was on target when he called ours the post-Christian era in the West; and the archbishop of Canterbury was not exaggerating when he suggested, "Let African and Asian missionaries come to England to help to convert the post-Christian heathenism in our country."

The apostles forecast that militant apostasy would eventually reach blasphemous proportions. St. Paul wrote that in the last days that there will be "blasphemers." St. Peter predicted that the very worst possible theological position the Church could take would be adopted by some. "There shall be false teachers among you, who privily shall bring in damnable heresies, even denying the Lord that bought them" (2 Peter 2:1). This to St. Peter (and St. Jude wrote almost exactly the same thing) was the absolute nadir. No one could go further down.

"People today," writes a churchman in a widely circulated Canadian magazine, "have no interest in the emotionalism of the cross and Christ's shed blood." One asks if men like these have experienced the efficacy of the cross. Obviously not. The tragedy, St. Peter further forecasts, would be that "they will gain many adherents to their dissolute practices, through whom the true way will be brought into disrepute" (2 Peter 2:2 NEB). As for the consequence to themselves, their "judgment now of a long time lingereth not, and their damnation slumbereth not" (2 Peter 2:3).

"Jesus was the son of a Roman soldier," writes one American bishop, and "to worship Christ" is "rank idolatry." Yet, even a non-churchman like Abraham Lincoln affirmed, "I know that liberty is right, for Christ teaches it, and Christ is God." It was also refreshing to hear the secular humanist Pierre Berton on the CBC "Journal" (Christmas, 1984) recall that when he was a boy, the birth of Jesus Christ the Son of God was what characterized Christmas. Today, however, it's a George Orwell-styled Santa Claus, and Berton laments the degradation.

If people in (or outside) the Church will not worship Jesus Christ as their Messiah, then they must construct some other messiah. An American churchman writes in a national magazine that Marshal Matt Dillon (Jim Arness) of "Gunsmoke," Ben Cartwright of "Bonanza" (Lorne Green), and "Ironside" (Raymond Burr), represent "Messiah-like" figures: "Each of these characters represents a fragment, however tiny, of Christ." Our Lord cautioned us about this, forecasting that prior to His coming: "If anyone says to you then, 'Look, here is Christ!' or, 'There he is!' don't believe it. False christs and false prophets are going to appear" (Matthew 24:23,24, Phillips). The aging apostle John was very emphatic that: "Every spirit that acknowledges the fact that Jesus Christ actually became man, comes from God, but the spirit which denies this fact does not come from God. The latter comes from the antichrist" (1 John 4:2,3, Phillips). When I was a lad, it was unheard of; but today, the world over, media people refer to many meteoric and magnetic personalities as "messiahs" with super "charisma."

Norm Perry on CTV's "Canada AM" asked in late 1984: Is Michael Jackson a "messiah," as many of his pop fans and fellow Jehovah Witness zealots claim? Peter Pockling-ton, owner of the Stanley Cup champion Edmonton Oilers, while running for the Conservative leadership of Canada, had a court-case run-in with Rita Burns, a psychic who contended what Pocklington did not deny, that he said, "Every day I look at myself in the mirror and say, 'You are a god. People do your will because you are a god.' " Robert Charlebois, the rock idol, is welcomed by his Ontario fans as being so "like a god." David Miller writes that the underlying reason why fifteen percent of our physicians are alcoholics or drug addicts is their inability to cope with the public perception of them as so "god-like." The messiah image is too much for them. They are not magicians. John Lynn writes of the World Series Super-Star as being im-mediately adulated by tens of millions as "someone to—wor-ship," but goes on to say that the messiah burden always turns from adulation to devastation, eventually.

Tolstoy stated that every man has in him a God-shaped blank. Another Russian, Dostoevsky, put it even more vividly,

"So long as man remains, he strives for nothing so incessantly and so painfully as to find someone to worship." If a nominal Christian rejects orthodox Christianity, he will not live in a religious vacuum. He will create a new religion, complete with messiah and the ritualistic trappings to go along with it. Erich Fromm, writing on the reason for outbreaks of violence, attributes it to Americans having in so many instances abandoned their Christian beliefs, and consequently being caught in the transition of searching for a replacement. Some "messiah" appears and they'll chase him, even though he is a charlatan.

Jesus saw people during His incarnation as He sees them today, fainting, scattered abroad, and as sheep without a shepherd. "Nothing reflects confusion more than a flock of sheep without a shepherd," wrote the late Dr. L. Nelson Bell (as executive director of *Christianity Today*). "Beset by barking dogs, frustrated by one another and by the natural obstacles around them, leaderless sheep will mill about in a frenzy of indecision, unable to cope with the problems that confront them." This is why every sheep demands a shepherd. It is why every man must have a messiah: real or imagined. A brilliant writer told me recently that he is convinced that everything a man does reflects his religious nature, for essentially he is chronically and eternally religious. He cited the current university craze: to establish departments of parapsychology in every sophisticated institution of higher learning, including those in the Soviet Union.

Finally, concerning the Church and the coming of Christ, two points need highlighting. The period preceding the second advent of Christ would be, for the Church, a time of unprecedented persecution and of great evangelistic harvest, for I do not believe that our Lord will come for an utterly defeated Church. It will be a time of grave persecution. In the last days, wrote St. Paul to Timothy, "Persecution is inevitable for those who are determined to live really Christian lives, while wicked and deceitful men will go from bad to worse" (2 Timothy 3:12,13, Phillips).

Time recently described how the Reds "are keeping in jail tens of thousands of Christians in Red China, Russia and other countries. They torture them. They take children away from their parents if they teach them Christianity." A *Reuter* report

(March 23, 1985) on the Church in Russia observes that there are "growing signs recently that hardline proponents of communist orthodoxy" are currently contending for a return to the "repression" of Christianity, as practiced by Josef Stalin. On the other hand, my conversations in places like Macao and Hong Kong with believers who had escaped out of China, convinced me that while the blood of the martyrs had been flowing in that land as it has perhaps in no country in history, the Church underground is flourishing. I am told that from, say, 1945 to 1985, the numbers of the "born again" in Red China have increased during a single generation from an estimated four million to forty million. My time in the Soviet Union and talks with Christians there have convinced me that, despite the widespread persecution, the numbers turning to Christ may well exceed anything in Russian history.

An interesting article appears in *Molodoi Kommunist,* the official paper of the Young Communist League of the Soviet Union. It laments that sixty percent of the babies born in the large industrial city of Gorki are being baptized. This may say little, or it may say much. A recent letter written to the pope by Anatoly Levitin, a Russian, contains thrilling accounts of the innumerable conversions of the young of his country to Jesus Christ in a revival which "in intensity and strength is no less than the feeling of fiery enthusiasm among the earliest Christians." Nor are these just peasants—as it has supposedly been in the past. "More and more frequently there are cases in Moscow where the sons of Communists and even of old Tchekists (security police) are baptized" as an outward demonstration of an inner spiritual revolution. Such baptisms in a Communist country require a great deal of courage on the part of the participants.

Certainly Billy Graham, after his fifty-two meetings across the Soviet countries and into Siberia, is convinced that Russian believers are both more in quantity and higher in quality than he would ever have otherwise believed. The Church under the pressure of persecution has always developed a stronger head of steam. East Germany is on a fresh campaign to curb Christianity—but it won't work. On average, East German Christians are far more dedicated and dynamic than those of West Germany.

The provinces of Orissa, Madhya and Pradesh in India have outlawed Christian witness, but from my talks with Christians in India I suspect it will only intensify the effectiveness of Christian testimony. Whether it is in Cuba, Egypt, Poland, or eventually right here in North America, persecution goads the Church into virility and true spirituality. "Be patient, my brothers, until the Lord comes," St. James entreated, for "the farmer looking for the precious crop his land may yield can only wait in patience, until the winter and spring rains have fallen. You too must be patient and stout-hearted, for the coming of the Lord is near" (James 5:7,8 NEB). Let us all pray for the latter or spring rains to fall.

An irony of our times is that while many church leaders are more and more agnostic, there has never been a time when such a high percentage of laymen believe that a spiritual revival is the need of our hour. *Fortune* magazine's poll of the American people reveals that fifty-three percent of U.S. businessmen are convinced that a "spiritual awakening is what their nation most needs."

An illuminating statistic is that, whereas in 1956 fifty-seven percent of the foreign missionary force of North American Protestantism was made up of representatives of the evangelical denominations and sects, it is now eighty percent and rising steadily. "Evangelicalism is where the action is," comments the *New York Times*.

I never watch the huge and sometimes almost unbelievable harvest of inquirers streaming down to the front in a Billy Graham Crusade, but . . . I think of the promise of St. Peter as recorded in Acts 3, "Repent therefore, and turn again, that your sins may be blotted out, that times of refreshing may come from the presence of the Lord, and that he may send the Christ appointed for you, Jesus" (Acts 3:19,20 RSV). When one realizes that Billy Graham in 1984—during that one year—expected a gathering of 1,800 at a ministers' meeting in England and, instead, witnessed a coming together of 11,000; packed the largest stadium in Alaska for eight nights; conducted Mission England, in which a million attended the six crusades, not in London but in the smaller provincial centers, with 100,000 making decisions for Christ; traveled to Korea where a million gathered in one meeting, with another ten million gathered around TV screens; held those fifty-two meetings across the Soviet Union; and led a crusade in the most commodious indoor sports stadium in the world, B.C. Place, where the largest evangelistic meeting in the history of Canada assembled: the harvest for the year of ministry was nothing short of a modern miracle, performed by the Holy Spirit! For our part, we who witnessed what happened when we assembled at the end of the year of ministry as a Billy Graham team, to rejoice at what God was doing—having seen as many as 5,000 a night making decisions for Christ, could only exclaim: "This is the Lord's doing and it is marvelous in our eyes."

Researchers tell us that, worldwide, 60,000 people daily—on average—are professing to be born again, 25,000 of these in Africa. The authority on world religions, Englishman David Barratt, estimates that in 1985 there are a half-billion "born-again" Christians worldwide. Were Christ to come again this moment, and the assessment were accurate, that would be the number of living people who would be airlifted to heaven. For those of us who anticipate that event, it will have no match for victory. For those left behind, it will mean the ushering in of the most tragic era in the history of man's long sojourn on Planet Earth.

In a cover story in *Time* the current born-again movement is unequivocably linked with the return of Christ; the twelve-page article is entitled: "The New Rebel Cry: Jesus is Coming!" The number of young turning to Christ in the seventies and eighties both in North America and throughout the world is unprecedented in the history of the Church. And there is more. *Time* exudes, "We are on the threshold of the greatest spiritual revival the U.S. has ever experienced." The prayer of the late Pope John XXIII was cited: "[Holy Spirit,]renew your wonders in this our day, as by a new Pentecost."

The *Time* article aligns the "Jesus Is Coming" movement not only with Billy Graham and associated crusades, the Jesus Movement, and the charismatics—both among Catholics and Protestants—but also with Campus Crusade for Christ, which currently has 3,000 full-time staffers on 450 university and college campuses; with Inter-Varsity Christian Fellowship, which assembled at the University of Illinois in December 1984 a missionary convention of 18,000 (a record); with Young Life, which has 1,300 clubs, U.S. and foreign, working chiefly with high schoolers; and with Youth for Christ, which has evangelism cells in 2,700 high schools throughout the world. It also states that, just when it seemed least likely, there is a whole new renewal movement within mainstream churches which had resisted revivalistic awakenings and evangelical theology for decades. Indeed, many denominations are finding a fresh river of blessing flowing through their ranks.

What is true in North America is even truer in other parts of the world, such as East and South Asia and the Island world. In South America, reportedly in a single year, the evangelical church rolls were enlarged by an incredible fifteen percent over the previous year. Dr. Paul Smith, returning from remarkable revival meetings in Brazil in March 1985, observed that, in that country, and indeed in several South American countries, there are actually more people being "born again" than "born." And it can happen in any part of the world. The church that turns to God in prayer can experience revival today as always, perhaps in a greater measure than ever before—"and so much the more as ye see the day approaching."

Chapter Six

Geopolitics and the Coming Christ

"To stand against Israel would be to stand against God," kibitzed Ted Kennedy to Jerry Falwell in 1983. Irritate modern secularists it may, but it does not alter what was well expressed in the words of Dr. Charles Malik, the first president of the United Nations General Assembly, that "to dismiss the present conflict between the children of Isaac and Ishmael [Israelis and the Arabs] as just an ordinary politico-economic struggle is to have no sense whatsoever of the holy and the ultimate in history."

It just so happens that, currently, the most powerful man on earth is President Ronald Reagan. Indeed, Dr. Helen Caldicott, the Harvard nuclear-freeze crusader, labels Reagan as the most powerful man in this century or perhaps in all of history (CBC interview, December 5, 1984). Apparently the reason President Reagan is so sensitive to the situation in the Middle East is because he believes the biblical prophecies. As *Time* (November 5, 1984) makes clear, the surest sign of the future advent of the Messiah, insofar as President Reagan and most evangelicals are concerned, is the restoration of Israel to the Jewish people. This began when Israel was officially proclaimed a nation in 1948, and, more specifically, when Israel repossessed Old Jerusalem in 1967.

Any true Christian believer in the twilight of the twentieth century has to ask some basic questions such as this one: Can a militantly atheistic philosophy such as communism, currently in control of one-third of the population of the earth, and persistently going as far as it dares to exterminate the faith of Jesus Christ and His Church, escape the ultimate judgment of God?

Victor Hugo pointed out that Western Europe and North America, as a result of their Christian character, have produced a varied orchard bearing the richest fruit in human history. Civilization, culture, education, wealth and technological advances—all in the wake of Christianity—have staggered the imagination. But the very Christianity which provided a base for all this has all too often been compromised and even apostatized. The church, particularly in Western Europe, has been abandoned by over ninety percent of the people. For the first time in centuries, every country simultaneously registers a distinct decline in Christian belief, according to the Gallup Poll. As both the pope in 1984 and Britain's archbishop of Canterbury point out, Europeans are witnessing the advent of the post-Christian era. Can such a state of affairs long escape the tyranny of an Antichrist? In such times, according to some, the Church will be driven underground, or, as in my view, it will be taken upward into heaven, withdrawn from the "wrath to come."

Our Lord forecast that prior to His coming again there would be "wars and rumors of wars." It was not only divinely prophesied, but such leaders as Douglas MacArthur, Dwight D. Eisenhower—currently, of course, President Reagan—and a vast array of leading writers and editorialists in such papers as the prestigious *London Times* with uniform regularity predict a coming Armageddon. According to a standard dictionary, the meaning of Armageddon is: "Place of great and final conflict between the forces of good and evil."

Obviously only a sweeping panorama of coming events such as that forecast in the Bible is possible here, and the *sine qua non* of scriptural prophecy remains the people of Israel. Increase Mather was president of Harvard from 1685 to 1701. At a time when Palestine was a desolate wilderness in the hands of the Turks and virtually devoid of Jews, Mather wrote in *The Mystery of Israel's Salvation Explained* with regard to the regathering of Israel to the ancient homeland, that "the Scripture is very clear and full in this, that you see not how it can be justly denied or questioned." Mather was so astonishingly perceptive concerning biblical prediction that he foresaw that "the Israelites at their return, shall even fly." Anyone who has recently been to Israel cannot escape seeing this happen on six out of seven days in Tel Aviv airport. The Englishman John Owen, thought of by many as the foremost of all Congregationalist ministers, wrote in 1673, "The Jews shall be gathered from all parts of the earth where they now are scattered, and brought home into their homeland." An anthology of such statements during every generation from A.D. 70 to the present could be written.

Why should Israel be the special object of Jehovah's regathering? Because God keeps His Word! It is as simple as that. In Genesis we read that God spoke to His friend Abraham, who put implicit faith in Him, and instructed, "Get thee out of thy country, and from thy kindred, and from thy father's house, unto a land that I will shew thee: and I will make of thee a great nation" (Genesis 12:1,2). When Abraham had obeyed God and left the comfortable nest which was Ur of the Chaldees and had gone into the land which is modern Israel, God again spoke to him and said, "And I will give unto thee, and to thy seed after thee, the land wherein thou art a stranger, all the land of Canaan, for an everlasting possession; and I will be their God" (Genesis 17:8). When God says, "Everlasting," one who believes the Scriptures has no good reason to state that that is not precisely what He meant. Moreover, He promised that such would be His covenant and fealty to Abraham's seed that "I will bless them that bless thee, and curse him that curseth thee" (Genesis 12:3).

That the Jewish people are the recipients of these promises was later indicated by the Lord's reappearance to Abraham to assure him, "In Isaac shall thy seed be called" (Genesis 21:12). For 430 years, Israel sojourned in the land of Egypt, but Moses led them back to the borders of their homeland and Joshua guided them in to possess it. After the apostasy during the times of the kings, Israel went into Babylonian captivity, but Nehemiah and Ezra were in the phalanx to lead them back.

In an Israel which had been occupied by foreign powers since Nebuchadnezzar's seige in 486 B.C., our Lord was born of a Hebrew virgin. A third of a century later, having come "unto his own, and his own received him not" (John 1:11), He was crucified. During the week of our Lord's crucifixion He

predicted that "all these things shall come upon this
generation." This was unmistakably the siege and utter destruction of Jerusalem by Titus of Rome in A.D. 70, in which many
Jews were massacred. Those who escaped fled to the ends of the
earth, a scattering from which they have only begun to return
during recent years. Jesus made it unmistakably plain, "And
they shall fall by the edge of the sword, and shall be led away
captive into all nations: and Jerusalem shall be trodden down of
the Gentiles, until the times of the Gentiles be fulfilled" (Luke
21:24). When it is realized that Jerusalem has been a city occupied by Gentiles until the Six-Day War in June 1967, it is evident that we are living in very exciting times indeed.

Meanwhile, from the time Peter was commissioned to in-
troduce the Gospel to the Gentiles by going to Cornelius and his
household, the Church of Jesus Christ has been constituted
chiefly of non-Jewish Christians. St. James argued to the
Jerusalem Assembly (Acts 15:14-16 NEB): "God took notice of
the Gentiles, to choose from among them a people to bear his
name; and this agrees with the words of the prophets, as Scripture has it. Thereafter I will return and rebuild the fallen house
of David; even from its ruins I will rebuild it, and set it up
again."

In St. Paul's letter to the Romans, chapters nine to eleven
are strikingly relevant. Keeping in mind that in the Acts of the
Apostles it is made quite plain that, because the Jews had rejected the Lord of glory and crucified Him, God had turned to
the Gentiles to regenerate a body of believers known as the
Church, Paul taught, "Through their [Israel's] fall, salvation is
come to the Gentiles." But this, he states, is a parenthesis. He
cautions Gentile believers that they are wild branches grafted into the true tree of God's chosen, but that as Israel has been set
aside, so shall she be taken up again: "You will say, 'Branches
were lopped off so that I might be grafted in.' Very well, they
were lopped off for lack of faith, and by faith you hold your
place. Put away your pride, and be on your guard; for if God
did not spare the native branches, no more will he spare you"
(Romans 11:19-21 NEB).

Paul goes on to say that "it is in God's power to graft them
in again. For if you were cut from your native wild olive and
against all nature grafted into the cultivated olive, how much

more readily will they, the natural olive-branches, be grafted into their native stock'' (Romans 11:24 NEB). In summing up,
Paul clarifies, ''There is a deep truth here, my brothers, of
which I want you to take account, so that you may not be com-
placent about your own discernment; this partial blindness has
come upon Israel only until the Gentiles have been admitted in
full strength; when that has happened, the whole of Israel will
be saved.'' In concluding, Paul declares, ''God's choice stands,
and they [Israel] are His friends for the sake of the patriarchs
[Abraham, Isaac and Jacob]'' (Romans 11:25, 26, 28 NEB).

The prediction is clear, and the immense amount of Old
Testament prophecy pertaining to the final restoration of Israel
to their ancient homeland becomes astonishingly meaningful.
For example, Isaiah, who devoted whole chapters to this theme,
is the Lord's oracle of prophecy: ''And it shall come to pass in
that day, that the Lord shall set his hand again the second time
to recover the remnant of his people from the four corners of
the earth'' and ''thy people . . . shall inherit the land [in
perpetuity]'' (Isaiah 11:11,12b; 60:21).

Three points here: ''again the second time'' can only refer to
a regathering of Israel *since* scriptural days, because the
recovery from Babylonian captivity was the only other one from
Isaiah's time to the present. Secondly, ''the four corners of the
earth'' or, as Jeremiah 32:37 puts it, ''Behold, I will gather
them out of all countries, whither I have driven them in mine
anger,'' can only refer realistically to the current return of
Israel, because any previous dispersions were merely to one or
only a few nations in the Middle East, certainly not to anything
like ''all countries'' in ''the four corners of the earth.'' Modern
Jews have returned to Israel from 107 countries, literally from
all over the world.

The third point is, ''Thy people shall inherit the land [in
perpetuity].'' As Amos put it, ''I will bring back the captivity of
my people, and they shall no more be plucked up out of their
land which I have given them, saith Jehovah thy God'' (Amos
9:14,15 ASV). This indicates that Israel will not be ''driven into
the sea'' as enemies have threatened to do to her, nor will
Jerusalem again become a part of a Gentile empire. It will be
overrun during the Great Tribulation and by the end of Armageddon almost entirely destroyed and renewed. But from

then on, Jerusalem will be Jewish. It is apparent that Israelis are moved to return to their ancient homeland by chauvinism and ethnic ties as much as by an attachment to Judaism. This is true, and precisely as the Scriptures predict. "In the latter days," prophesied Hosea, "shall the children of Israel return, and seek the Lord their God, and David their king" (Hosea 3:5). The sequence is that they would return, largely in unbelief, as St. Paul taught, and would begin to seek their Messiah when settled. At the Revelation of Jesus Christ, a "nation will be born in a day," and as W. A. Criswell, a president of the Southern Baptist Convention, declared at a Jerusalem Conference on Bible Prophecy, there and then would be realized the "happy prospect" that Israel will "repent over her rejection of the One she pierced, the Lord Jesus Christ." When our Lord was born, His coming was to witness "the fall and rising again of many in Israel" (Luke 2:34). Note the order. Israel would "fall" and be scattered, but she would "rise" again. Histories of other nations may be entitled *Rise and Fall*, . . . but for Israel it would be *Fall and Rise*. . . .

In turning to a précis of events pertaining to Israel's restoration, such a volume of evidence has accumulated over the last few years and is even now accumulating at such a pace that the phenomenon almost staggers an objective observer. I happened to be preaching in the Peoples Church, Toronto, on the Sunday night in June 1967 when rumblings of the Six-Day War indicated that the Middle East was breaking out in flames. As Levi Eshkol, the Israeli prime minister, pointed out, Israel could only get scattered snatches of arms (their tanks were World War I vintage and apparently obsolete). They were outnumbered forty to one by Arabs with armies that were outfitted with Russia's best and that had repeatedly resolved to drive them into the Mediterranean. In the teeth of these overwhelming odds against Israel, I read on that occasion Luke 21:24, in which Jesus stated that when God's time for the return of Christ was drawing nigh, Jerusalem would no longer be trodden down by non-Jews. On the basis of Jesus' statement, I intimated that it should not surprise any Bible believer if, within hours, the Israelis were again in possession of Jerusalem never again to be expelled. In a matter of six days, this and much more was history. The geographical size of Israel was suddenly quadrupled. *Time* pointed out that the repossession of Old Jerusalem by Israel was a fulfillment of a biblical prophecy that had to occur before the second coming of Christ—a fact that the last four, if not five, U.S. presidents have agreed is a tenet of the prophetic Scriptures. One of President Reagan's earliest resolves was this one: "First, I believe that this nation has a moral obligation and commitment to the preservation of the nation of Israel."

It was my honour to appear on a Canadian television network program with Norm Perry and with Dr. Case, president of the Association of Orthodox Jewish Scientists in Canada. Asked if, as a scholar, he believed in miracles, Dr. Case went into careful detail to point out that the whole existence and expansion of the modern state of Israel has to be a miracle. There simply is no other explanation for it.

The Bible predicted that Jews would be "hated of all nations." How else can you explain Hitler's extermination of some six million Jews? Alexander Solzhenitsyn astounded the world by revealing that Stalin's death could best be explained by stating that it was a direct judgment on him for his newly contrived plan to systematically slaughter all remaining Jews in Russia, having already exterminated some seven million.

We, the Billy Graham team, feel so strongly the wrong of atrocities against the Jews that two of our main films have been *His Land*, which is about Israel, and *The Hiding Place*, which depicts how the Dutch sisters Corrie and Betsie ten Boom exercised their Christian love in Holland during World War II by giving themselves to rescuing and preserving Jews from the Gestapo. For doing so, Betsie and her aged father were put to death in the cruelest and crudest manner imaginable.

One of my Jewish neighbors said to me one day, "Everyone is out to get us. Why us?" Look at the votes in the United Nations. Only three times in my memory has it been lopsided in the extreme. In 1956, when the Israeli-Egyptian crisis arose, seventy-one countries voted against Israel; one voted in her favour. When the United Nations voted in 1967 on whether Israel should retain possession of Jerusalem, which they regained after the Six-Day War, the vote was: sixty-nine against, none for. When the matter of quelling Shiite terrorists in Southern Lebanon in March 1985 came up before the U.N., Israel, in its efforts to put down the guerrillas at the Lebanon-

Israel frontier again received only one vote (*Reuter*, March 13, 1985). Is it any wonder that two-thirds of the Israeli budget is earmarked for defense!

Despite the ecumenical movement with all of its ironic "goodwill" overtures, Rabbi Emil Fackenheim reckons reflectively that Christian denominations are more antagonistic toward Jews today than they have ever been in history. Editorializes the *Toronto Star* (March 7, 1985): "The future of Jerusalem is one of the most contentious issues" in the world today. Every state in the world has very strong views on the Jewish people in general, and Jerusalem in particular.

What makes the Israeli state more miraculous is the fact that never in history has a country gone out of existence and come back to life after a burial of even 500 years, let alone 2,500. One hundred and thirty years ago, Jerusalem had a population of 3,000 Jews, and in all of Palestine there were 8,000. Sixty years ago, there were still only 41,000 Jews in Palestine; even after World War II, there were only half a million. Today there are 3.6 million, and Yitzhak Shamir visits in Canada, pleading for more Jews to "come home" (*Toronto Sun*, March 18, 1985).

Despite runaway inflation Israel is one of only six nations on earth which produces more food than their home market consumes. One has to see Israel to believe that this land, until recently a barren wilderness, is such a flourishing garden today. In the words of the ancient Ezekiel, as he interpets that valley of dry bones parable: "This land that was desolate is become like the garden of Eden; and the waste and desolate and ruined cities are become fenced, and are inhabited" (Ezekiel 36:35).

The fact that the Jews would migrate back to Palestine with the scriptural conviction that this was inevitable came very much to the fore among Protestant theologians in the nineteenth century. This paved the way for the political possibilities. Simultaneously, Jews all over the world were being fascinated by Theodor Herzl's Zionist Movement which sought to stir support for a restoration of Palestine to homecoming Jews. In 1917, General Allenby of Britain captured Jerusalem from the Turks without firing a shot, and, in November of that year, the Balfour Declaration made it possible for the Jewish people to settle unharrassed (at least in name) in their ancient homeland. In October 1947, the great powers felt guilty enough to try to compensate Israel for what Nazi Germany had done and rallied support in the United Nations to give Israel a charter to become a sovereign and independent state. And so, in May 1948, Israel became a sovereign state for the first time in 2500 years.

"The Bible," asserted the late David Ben-Gurion, "is our mandate." It is not insignificant that the former prime minister of Israel gave the opening speech to the Jerusalem Conference on Bible Prophecy, other speakers being evangelicals. UPI newsman George Cornell notes, "In Italy, it's the opera. In Switzerland, it's the Alps. In Russia, it's the Party. In America, it's baseball. But in Israel, it's the Bible. It's the people's principal pastime." They search its pages for guidance in every detail for the restoration of "the land." Joshua Cohen writes in the *Toronto Star* that "what the world in general, and Israel in particular, today needs is not basically a materialist solution to their problems. Guns and money don't always save countries, empires or people. Our Bible saved us; could still save the world too, if it followed the Bible. Try it."

Modern Israel has only one-three-hundredth of the population that modern China has, yet this tiny nation gets three times the headlines around the world. Why? Because it is the hinge country on which the world swings. History began in the Middle East and it will end there. There is no point at which scriptural prediction and current events so exactly coincide as on this Jewish issue. The newspapers are replete with it. Whether you read the headlines, the editorials, letters to the editor, the religion or the financial page, statements abound such as in the *Toronto Star*—in which it is declared that this little land has "expanded beyond pre-1967 Israel's wildest dreams." Jewish people, wherever they may live in the world, have a fierce love and allegiance for Israel; whenever opposition to their cause arises, they close ranks rapidly. *Time* quotes Israel's leaders as wanting a million more workers immediately, and while other nations want to reduce their population growth, Israel is working on doubling hers in the next decade.

I shall never forget arriving in Jerusalem on the eve of the first New Year in 2500 years that the Israelis were in occupation and in sovereign control of their capital. I have never felt such electric expectation—the air teemed with it. Crowds rejoicing and weeping for joy were everywhere. The ram's horn was ready to blast out the sound that Messiah had come. The old Wailing Wall, bared down seventeen stone levels, was the scene of indescribable festivities and anticipation! I felt that until that moment I, like most Christians, was unable to grasp what power there is in revived and expectant Judaism. It is currently being asked whether or not Israel will relinquish Jerusalem again to any other power. The answer of every premier—from Mrs. Golda Meir to Peres and Shamir—is, absolutely, absolutely not! As Jerusalem mayor Teddy Kollek makes clear: Jews are in Israel—and in Jerusalem in particular—"until the Messiah returns" (*Reuter*, March 23, 1985). Even interest in a restoration of the Temple is now quickening. Immediately prior to the Six-Day War, when Old Jerusalem was taken, the *Washington Post* (May 21) ran this astonishing quarter-page advertisement: *To Persons of the Jewish Faith All Over the World:* "A Project to Rebuild the Temple of God in Israel is now being started. With Divine Guidance and Help, the 'Temple' will be completed. It will signal a new era in Judaism. Jews will be inspired to conduct themselves in such a moral way that our Maker will see fit to pay us a visit here on earth. . . . Executive talent, administrators, and workers on all levels are needed. . . . God will know those desiring to participate." A box number was given. According to Defense Minister Moshe Dayan, there will eventually be an extension of Israel's "frontiers to where they belong" to include all "the land between the Nile and the Euphrates."

Few internationalists would argue otherwise than that *London Times* is the world's premier English newspaper. In a syndicated article by David Lundy and Hirsh Goodman, carried in hundreds of newspapers throughout the world (including the *Toronto Star,* October 7, 1984) under headlines such as "Pursuit of Armageddon,""Paving the Way for Doomsday"and "Israeli [Plan to] Clear Way for Messiah," the article begins. "Ezekiel's vision of God's apocalyptic prophecies are ominously relevant in Jerusalem at a time when 20 men stand accused in the biggest trial of Jewish terrorists in the history of the state of Israel. The men are accused of [the] illegal possession of huge arms caches, [having] plotted to blow up the Dome of the Rock mosque in Jerusalem. [These] accused believe, on the strength of biblical interpretation, that the mosque is an 'abomination' and that its destruction will [prepare the way for] the coming of the Messiah. [These] men on trial are not a part of a lunatic fringe, but are leaders of the Jewish establishment; [actually] Israeli Defense Force officers and a former fighter pilot. Their messianic fervor, if not [always] the violent means they employ, is shared [by] orthodox Israeli Jews [in] alliance [with] 43 million U.S. fundamentalists [plus Canadian evangelicals] in the growing belief that the end is imminent. 'The world is ready for the final curtain.' " The article goes on to say that the accused believe, with varying degrees of conviction that, in the words of "Lambert Dolphin, a physicist from Stanford Research Institute [that] 'The Temple Mount is probably the hottest piece of archaelogical real estate in the world'; [that the Moslem Mosque] The Dome of the Rock . . . built in A.D. 691 [must be removed, regardless how inflamed the Islamic world may become]. Christians believe the rock is where Abraham came to sacrifice Isaac and where Jesus taught. It is the site [of] Solomon's temple, built there in 950 B.C.; a second temple was destroyed by the Romans. [These people] believe that after the destruction of the mosque, construction of a third temple [will] begin and this will herald the Second Coming. [Orthodox Jewish Scholar and] architect, 83-year-old Jacob Yehuda, has researched the plans of the third temple [based on] Ezekiel, chapters 40, 41 and 42. [The Israeli Government conducting this trial, understandably in extreme secrecy, all] evidence has been presented in camera. [The order of events is that when, and however it happens, the Dome of the Rock is destroyed, this will bring on the Moslem world, led by the Shiite Iranians—Persia, the Libyans and Ethiopians, to be incited by the Soviets in what Orthodox Jews call the Gog-Magog War of Ezekiel 38 and 39. At any moment the Middle East could erupt into a [nuclear] conflict that will be the war of annihilation [of] Russia and her allies by the Israelis [when the Soviets] will suffer an overwhelming defeat; when five-sixths of their invading army will be destroyed." A careful reading of Ezekiel 38 and 39 describes this horrific holocaust, according to Orthodox Jews and Bible-believing Christians. A passage is cited at the opening of this *London Times* article which I had never before noticed, "And I looked, and, behold, a whirlwind came out of the north, a great cloud, and a fire infolding itself" (Ezekiel 1:4).

Is Russia in biblical prophecy? It is—most precisely in Ezekiel 38 and 39, and also in both Daniel 11 and Revelation 20. Certainly, as the leader of world communism, Russia has been at the fore of Communist-incited revolutions for a half-century now, revolutions that have changed the face of the earth's political geography and the whole course of twentieth-century history. Jesus forewarned us that prior to His coming again there would be "wars and revolutions." The communization of Eastern Europe occurred as a result of the Soviets' opportunism late in World War II and the compromises the Western Allies were prepared to make with Stalin—just for peace. Within four years, nearly another one-fourth of the human race fell to the Communist Revolution in China. Since 1950, the Korean and Vietnam Wars dragged on and on, with half of Korea and all of Vietnam—along with Laos and Cambodia—going Communist, as Cuba did earlier. Ethiopia became full-fledged Communist in September 1984; Syria and Libya, and for all intents and purposes Iran, moved into accord with the Soviets (as prophesied in Ezekiel 38:5). Afghanistan was simply conquered and occupied.

So powerful is the Communist war machine currently that, in the mid-eighties, the liberal *Toronto Star* (December 3, 1984) pauses long enough from its routine softness on Marxism to editorialize that, yes, "The Soviets [have] a decided political and military edge." The Soviets have many more missiles than does the U.S., they're more advanced in anti-satellite technology, and their armed forces vastly outgun NATO's in Europe. Ilya Gerol, a longtime Soviet journalist until his defection to Canada, wrote in 1982 of Mikhail Gorbachev that he was a hardliner who bore watching. Although he has a pleasing personality, underneath is a will of tungston-hard steel and a commitment to the conquest of the world by communism. In the 38th and 39th chapters of Ezekiel, the details are amazingly explicit. It should be kept in mind that these chapters follow directly Ezekiel's vision of the valley of dry bones, which the prophet interprets, "Thus saith the Lord God: Behold, O my people, I will open your graves, and cause you to come up out of your graves, and bring you into the land of Israel"; and, "I will make them one nation in the land upon the mountains of Israel." Then in chapter 38 we read, "Son of man, set thy face toward Gog, of the land of Magog, the prince of Rosh,

Meshech, and Tubal, and prophesy against him, and say, Thus saith the Lord Jehovah, Behold, I am against thee.''

There is linguistic proof that this passage refers to Russia. ''Magog'' is mentioned in Genesis 10:2, and, according to Josephus, his descendants were the Scythians who migrated to the north, over the Caucasus between the Caspian and Black Seas into what is now Russia. In the evolution of ancient proper nouns into their modern derivatives, it is usual for the consonant sounds generally to remain, while the vowels frequently undergo change. Therefore, Rosh is commonly reckoned by lexicographers to be Russia; Tubal is thought to be the Asiatic province of Russia, Tobolski; and Meshech, Moscow. M. C. Wren's *Ancient Russia* (New York, 1965) makes apposite reading here.

Further evidence that these chapters refer to Russia is the fact that, as with the Daniel passage, their hordes came from ''the uttermost part of the north.'' The atheistic philosophy which impels them would be another indicator. Ezekiel refers to them as ''the heathen.'' A headline in the editorial section of the *Toronto Star* reads, ''Stalin's Shadow Again Darkens the Soviet Union.'' The article shows that the hard line of militarism and atheism is again being followed (see *Toronto Star*, March 23, 1985).

The ancient prophet Ezekiel states that this power will resolve to ''go up to the land of unwalled villages . . . all of them dwelling without walls, and having neither bars nor gates, to take a spoil, and to take a prey . . . [from] the people that are gathered out of the nations'' (Ezekiel 38:11,12). This ''people'' unmistakably refers to restored Israel. ''In that day when my people of Israel dwelleth safely . . . thou shalt come from thy place out of the north parts, thou, and many people with thee,'' [the Soviet Union has many Communist satellites] ''. . . a great company, and a mighty army: and thou shalt come up against my people of Israel, as a cloud to cover the land; it shall be in the latter days'' (vv. 14-16). This is a striking statement, but scarcely more so than the one in the following verse, after the explanation ''that the heathen [what could be more heathen than atheistic communism?] may know me . . . before their eyes. Thus saith the Lord God; Art thou he of whom I have spoken in old time by my servants the prophets of Israel, which prophesied in those days many years?" (v.17). In short, fulfilled prophecy always vindicates the character and authority of God.

Russian communism baffles its watchers. Winston Churchill sighed, "I cannot forecast to you the action of Russia. It is a riddle, wrapped in a mystery, inside an enigma." "Treaties are only for getting breath for a new effort. They exist to be broken as soon as expedient. Peace propaganda is to camouflage war preparations," insisted Lenin. It was hardly unexpected that President Reagan should say that the Soviets have "publicly declared that the only morality they recognize is what will further their cause, meaning they reserve unto themselves the right to commit any crime, to lie, to cheat in order to attain that." He later explained, "They don't subscribe to our idea of morality. They don't believe in a God or a religion, and the only morality they recognize, therefore, is what will advance the world of socialism." When Mr. Reagan was a guest of Prime Minister Mulroney during the "Shamrock Summit" in March 1985, he pointed to Ethiopia which was in the throes of a killer famine. While the U.S. gave $100 million to the starving there, the Soviets gave nearly nothing in terms of food: rather they gave their client Colonel Mariam $2 billion in armaments, many of which were used to attempt to starve into subjection those Ethiopians who resisted the tightening shackles of Marxism. Militarism? Yes! Morality? No!

So, as Ezekiel prophesied unmistakably, these invaders from the "uttermost part of the north" sweep down through what must be modern Syria "upon the mountains of Israel." It is important to note here, as *Time* points out, that Syria is a satellite of the Soviets and in 1981 was accepted into membership in the Warsaw Pact. It is governed by the Baath Party, which is Marxist both in origin and current commitment. The Russians have armed Syria to the hilt since 1957—they have some 5,000 Russian advisers at every level in Syria today, but most intensively in the military. So it is quite conceivable that the route the Soviets take will be through Syria. As reported in *Time*, the prime minister of Israel reckons that the most belligerent of Israel's Arab adversaries are the Syrians, who have been keeping, and will continue to keep, the Arab/Israeli conflict at a brink-of-war pitch at all times. When the war was raging in Lebanon, the AP was diligent to report that the Syrians acted only in concert with their Soviet backers.

Working in alliance with Russia will be Persia (Iran), Libya, and Ethiopia (Ezekiel 38:5). It is almost uncanny the way these three nations have fallen into the Soviet sphere, along with Syria, in the last twenty years. As President Reagan calls them, they are "surrogates of the Soviets." It is not without significance that, throughout the 1980s, world attention has been focused in turn, and again and again, on these three nations—Iran, Libya, and Ethiopia. The West had no more loyal ally than the Shah, but Iran had to change sides to fit Ezekiel 38:5, and it did so with a vengeance. The Ayatollah Khomeini's Shiite revolution with all of its bloody gore has been in the world headlines for years. His war with Iraq, which has killed at least a millon and which neither side seems to want to resolve, Khomeini named "Operation Jerusalem"—representing his intent not to stop until the ancient city is Islamic Shiite. The Iranian Shiites, of course, have been the sword of Mohammed in Lebanon, killing 239 American Marines in 1983 in one fell swoop, and another hundred Israelis, French and Americans since, in suicide raids. They are the incessant agitators on the Lebanon-Israeli borderland, keeping the state of affairs in constant turmoil.

And Libya—Gaddafi has vowed to die in Galilee, personally fighting in the war that would annihilate the "Zionists" once and for all and forever from the face of the earth. The news media space he has occupied with his paranoia-dominated rhetoric against Israel, the Sovietization of his military, and his verging on utterly insane tactics—all these things indicate that if the Middle East time bomb requires someone to eventually light the nuclear fuse, Gaddafi would count it the honor of a lifetime to do so—at any time!

The third member of this troika is Ethiopia which, with its seven million starving people suffering slow death in a famine which is not far short of a holocaust, has been the news story of late 1984. Dr. Keith Griffin of Oxford University, in a two-page article in the *Toronto Star* (December 1, 1984) lays the blame squarely at the feet of the Communist hardliner Mengistu Haile Mariam who, in the words of the *Star*, "turned Ethiopia upsidedown politically." In September 1984, ten years after leading Ethiopia into the socialist camp, Mariam spends $200 million (a *Wall Street Journal* estimate) celebrating his country's emergence as a full Marxist-Communist state, using every dollar or grain of wheat that he can lay his hands on to equip his army, feed them, and put down opposition. The great French philosopher Jean-François Revel, in his best seller *How Democracies Perish*, points to "the Marxist blood baths of [Chairman] Mariam in Ethiopia during the late 1970s" as a tragic example of how little the West cares (see *Time*, December 3, 1984). At the drop of a hat, Mariam will march with the Soviets on Israel. His wrath was aroused in 1985 when it was brought before the world that half of the 25,000 Falasha Jews of Ethiopia had been evacuated to Israel. The airlifts continue, aided by the C.I.A., among others. This will further enrage Mariam against Israel. So the Soviets will attack Israel. Why didn't it happen in 1982, when the Soviets were in Lebanon, on the doorstep of Israel? Because, as *Time* affirms, the Israelis have 200 neutron bombs on cruise missiles, ringed around Jericho, each aimed at a strategic Soviet or Arab capital. Fearing nuclear retaliation the Soviets have held back. But will they hold back for long? Ezekiel prophesied that the Soviets eventually shall, "think an evil thought: and thou shalt say, I will go up to the land of unwalled villages [Israel] . . . to take a spoil, and to take a prey; to turn thine hand upon the desolate places, that are now inhabited" (Ezekiel 38:10-12). Even more emphatically than evangelical Christians, Orthodox Jews believe that Israel is facing the inevitable showdown with the Soviets—to be known as "the Gog-Magog War." Earlier in the 1980s UPI carried news stories around the world of the three distinguished Jewish rabbis who had dreams on the same night that the Gog-Magog War was near. Noted the UPI report, "The Chief Rabbi of the Wailing Wall in Jerusalem's Old City is sure Israel will confront the Soviet Union in a battle over the Holy City. 'And it will be a nuclear war,' they contended, 'drawing in both superpowers.' "

The biggest news story of 1985 is "Star Wars," which means "war in heaven." It is my belief that this will be a nuclear exchange which will involve "fire and brimstone"—perhaps "particle beams"—rained down from above. And God's interventionist judgment on the Soviets and their allies will be to "turn thee back, and leave but the sixth part of thee, [and] seven months shall the house of Israel be burying of them, that they may cleanse the land. [Nuclear cleansing with its fallout is an incredible job; but the whole post-nuclear-process will take] . . . seven years" (Ezekiel 38:22; 39:2,12,9).

This is one of several reasons I believe the Gog-Magog War will take place at the beginning of what Jesus called the "Great Tribulation" (Matthew 24:29), with "seven years" to follow. The Church of all the ages will have been raptured to heaven (as taught in 1 Thessalonians 4:13-18). What will embolden the Soviets will be the absence of a half-billion born-again Christians (Anglican scholar David Barrat's estimate), including tens of thousands of North American leaders in the White House, the Senate, the Congress, the House of Commons, the military and elsewhere.

The nuclear exchange at that point, as I understand it, will kill one-third of the population of the earth (Ezekiel 38,39 and Revelation 9:18). I believe, along with the above quoted "Rabbi of the Wailing Wall" that it will be a "nuclear war," and that by far the largest losses will be in the heaviest populated areas of the U.S.S.R. and the U.S.A. (including Canada's cities along the American border). Thereafter the two principle superpowers would be decimated and room would be made for the Antichrist.

Highlighting such a terrible prospect for purposes of warning the world was *The Day After*, which on November 20, 1983, "commanded the largest audience ever to view a film" on TV—some 100 million people (*Toronto Star*, November 24, 1983). *The Day After* alluded to the 8th and 9th chapters of Revelation where we read of "fire, brimstone and smoke [radiation?] killing one-third of all mankind. [What] appeared to be a huge burning mountain was thrown into the sea destroying a third of all ships, and a third of the fish died [and] a great flaming star fell from heaven upon a third of the rivers and springs . . . poison[ing] a third of all the water on the earth." There was a "blazing like a torch, fell from the sky [dimming] the sun," "the moon," "the stars," so that they "turned dark" (Revelation 9:18; 8:9,10,12). That's exactly the scenario scientists Carl Sagan, Paul Ehrlich, and 15,000 others depicted in their petition for a nuclear freeze (*Reuter*, November 11, 1983; *Time*, November 14, 1983) and in their terrifying warnings on "The

Phil Donahue Show'' (November 11, 1983), e.g., the darkness, the one-third death toll in the first nuclear exchange, and the death in the oceans of the world.

Perhaps the Soviet side also should be quoted. Dr. Frank Sommers, a Toronto psychiatrist and chairman of Physicians For Social Responsibility, reported during a trip to Russia, ''A Soviet survey predicted a third of all humanity would be killed'' in a nuclear exchange (the same figure used by Albert Einstein and projected by the aged Apostle John—*Toronto Star*, June 28, 1983). But what would it take to trigger such a catastrophe? The World Assembly for Peace and Life and Against Nuclear War—convened in Prague—voiced the thinking of 2,500 delegates from 132 countries: ''Humanity stands at a crucial cross-roads of history. One step in the wrong direction—and the world could be irrevocably thrown into the abyss of nuclear war.''

Dr. Eric Fawcett, professor of Physics at the University of Toronto, writes: ''Nuclear war is likely in the near future—possibly a holocaust but probably a limited nuclear exchange, or perhaps an isolated accident. [This] fact [will] continue to be almost universally ignored [or denied] until it forces itself on humanity. [The] most hopeful consequence will be that many people will become instant peace activists, demanding an end to this intolerable threat to everything they love and hold dear. The most fearful consequence of this response will be political repression and social control by governments afraid of losing popular support, leading to a rigid Orwellian world.''

And happen it will: sooner or later. The consequent nuclear holocaust will make room for the Antichrist to rise out of the European Confederacy of Ten Nations—a recrudescence of the ancient Roman Empire—very much resembling, if not coinciding, with the current European Common Market. The ECC, of course, has expanded into the current ''ten'' from ''six'' at the beginning of the 1980s; *Time* observes that Europe has achieved her ''greatest unity since the beginning of the breakup of Charlemagne's Empire in 814.'' By 1984, the ECC had its own passport and through its own official organ *Europe Magazine* was carrying on a constant campaign to have its own army and strong man. So now the ECC is more and more politicizing, through its European Parliament.

In 1985, for the first time, a clear "majority of European Community residents" support "the 10—nation alliance [being] transformed into a 'United States of Europe' " (AP, January 18, 1985). It is also significant that the first head of the European Parliament was the Holocaust survivor, Jewess Simone Veil, to whom a Canadian network newscaster referred as a "political messiah." ECC talks more and more of militarizing by absorbing (with adaptations) NATO into its ranks. So the scenario for the emergence of the Antichrist is becoming more and more apparent.

In 1984 West German Chancellor Helmut Kohl joined Prime Minister Margaret Thatcher of Britain and the current president of the European Common Market, President François Mitterand of France, in appealing for a "politically and economically united Europe [as] man's march to the precipice has accelerated" (*Toronto Star*, March 18, 1984). This was the thinking, as the European Parliament (of 458) and the ten leaders of the "Community" met in Brussels. "Leadership, leadership!" exclaims former prime minister Edward Heath. This is what has to emerge from the European Common Market. Ten to save it and the world from catastrophe (*London Daily Telegraph,* February 13, 1984).

It was very significant that, in his cover-story feature in *Time* (March 5, 1984), Henry Kissinger writes a six-page essay on the absolute imperative that a "statesman" emerge in Western Europe to unify the military and political divergences in order to face down Soviet "intransigence." (Kissinger is clear that the U.S. must decrease and Europeanization increase dramatically, both militarily and politically, if there is to be hope for the avoidance of nuclear war in Europe. The "Leader" Kissinger describes has got to be a "peace propagandist" as well as a military and political genius. Press reports constantly come out on the possibilities of a nuclear holocaust collapsing democracy, especially in Western Europe, and a super-dictator rising up to rule with "authority" and "order." Some Bible scholars believe that when the "ten" expand, one of those joining countries will produce the Antichrist, ascending initially, of course, as a man of peace (Daniel 7:8,24). Potential entrants are Spain, Portugal and Austria—with Denmark, Greece and Ireland speaking often of leaving. *Time* (December

3, 1984) features the brilliant French philosopher/journalist Jean-François Revel's latest best seller, *How Democracies Perish*. Revel contends that "the era of Modern Democracy [on] the stage of world history is almost over." That is surely what the Bible teaches!

The readiness of many in the last quarter of the twentieth century to clamour for a super-dictator—yes, for an Antichrist—could be seen in their going to see the Rome-based film *The Antichrist*. Then North Americans went for *The Omen* as the film of the year, as they had earlier gone for *The Exorcist* and then for its sequel, *Damien*. *Time* states that "*The Omen* presents . . . a prophecy about the return of the Prince of Darkness, taken from Revelation to fit certain events of our time—the creation of Israel and the Common Market. [It then] argues persuasively that if Satan were to return in disguise," a certain terrifying world situation would prevail. The author of the article wonders darkly if there really might be "faith in these secular times to believe in a reincarnated devil," that is, the Antichrist.

However much attention is being given in the secular world to the Antichrist, much more explicit attention is given to him in Scripture where he is depicted not as a figment of the imagination but as a factual reality—a terrible personification of evil who will work more wholesale havoc than any other human being in the history of the world. The Apostle John, who makes several references, states in his first mention of the Antichrist that in "the last hour of the current age . . . antichrist is coming" (cf., 1 John 2:18). Jesus told His disciples that previous to His coming to earth to judge the nations and set up His kingdom, men would "see standing in the holy place 'the abomination that causes desolation,' spoken of through the prophet Daniel—let the reader understand" (Matthew 24:15 NIV).

So we turn to Daniel's description. Here we discover that the Antichrist is a man who arrogates to himself power—wicked, sinister, wonder-working power—and he does just as Jesus said he would do. Halfway through his reign he enters into the temple of God (by that time restored) and desecrates the altar, thereby breaking the covenant he had made with Israel to maintain their peaceful existence. His diabolical dictatorship is realized; the tyranny of terror becomes a reality. He shows himself to have been the most monstrous wolf in sheep's clothing in history as he sets out to conquer the world. Daniel sets the last half of the Antichrist's dominance at three-and-a-half years, which means that, in all, he will be on the scene for approximately seven years after his revelation. In the middle of his reign, we read, "He shall cause the sacrifice and the oblation to cease, and for the overspreading of abominations he shall make it desolate, even unto the consummation" [the return of Jesus Christ to the earth] (Daniel 9:27). "And from the time that the daily sacrifice shall be taken away, and the abomination that maketh desolate set up, there shall be a thousand two hundred and ninety days" (Daniel 12:11: St. John in Revelation times it as forty-two months). The Antichrist will not so much deny the existence of God, which communism does, as he will deny His authority. "Antichrist," wrote St. John, "denieth the Father and the Son" for "whosoever denieth the Son, the same hath not the Father" (1 John 2:22,23). He "shall do according to his will; and he shall exalt himself, and magnify himself above every god," foretold Daniel, "and shall speak marvelous things against the God of gods, and shall prosper till the indignation be accomplished: for that that is determined shall be done. Neither shall he regard the God of his fathers, nor the desire of women, nor regard any god: for he shall magnify himself above all. But in his estate shall he honor the god of forces: and a god whom his fathers knew not shall he honor with gold, and silver, and with precious stones, and pleasant things" (Daniel 11:36-38).

We see on television sets supersuds, superboy, superlight, supermouse, superman, superstars, and a *Time* cover feature on "Stars and Anti-Stars." While there is obviously nothing intrinsically wrong with these usages, they portend a preconditioning for the acceptance of the Antichrist when he comes. Everywhere there is a craving for authority and order. During the post-World War II era, more than half of the world's governments have been overthrown by coups d'état. Warns the United Nations Secretary-General, "I do not wish to seem overdramatic, but I can only conclude from the information that is available to me as Secretary-General that the members of the United Nations have perhaps ten years left in which to subordinate their ancient quarrels and launch a global partnership to curb the arms race, to improve the human environment, to defuse the population explosion, and to supply the required momentum to world development efforts." The alternative would lead to a worldwide scenario "beyond our capacity to control."

Shortly before his death, Bertrand Russell said that we must very soon have either world government or universal annihilation. He was right. Dr. Henri Spaak, the world-famous statesmen from Belgium, has expressed how crucially man needs a superstatesman. "The truth is that the method of international committees has failed," he reasons, and "the highest order of experience" indicates that only a world ruler can control the world. "Let him come, and let him come quickly . . . galvanize all governments . . . let him vanquish" anarchy from the earth. Roy Fuller, a poetry professor at Oxford, argues eloquently how close Europe and America are to a dictatorship. The late Cambridge historian Arnold Toynbee reckoned that man in his present panic is "ripe for the deifying of any new Caesar who might succeed in giving the world unity and peace."

In four of the five New Testament books St. John wrote, he refers to the coming Antichrist. In each of his three epistles John uses the term "antichrist," and in the Revelation, where John traces his rise, reign of terror, and demise in considerable detail, the apostle calls him the "Beast." St. Paul describes the Antichrist as the "man of sin." History began with the sin of man and closes with the "man of sin." As St. John described how he had taught a good deal about the coming Antichrist ("as ye have heard"), so St. Paul parenthesizes his description of this coming vile dictator with the reminder to the Thessalonians that, when he was with them, he had treated this theme in depth: "You cannot but remember that I told you this while I was still with you" (2 Thessalonians 2:5 NEB). So apparently a great deal was said about the Antichrist in apostolic preaching.

Before we mention a restricted number of salient features of the rule of the coming Antichrist, let us explore St. Paul's treatment of this "man of sin" in 2 Thessalonians 2. He is to "be revealed, the son of perdition" (verse 3, KJV). "He is the Enemy. He rises in his pride against every god, so called, every object of men's worship, and even takes his seat in the temple of God claiming to be a god himself." Paul further explains. "You must now be aware of the restraining hand which ensures that he shall be revealed only at the proper time. For already the secret power of wickedness is at work, secret only for the present until the Restrainer disappears from the scene. And then he will be revealed, that wicked man whom the Lord Jesus will destroy with the breath of his mouth, and annihilate by the radiance of his coming. But the coming of that wicked man is the work of Satan. It will be attended by all the powerful signs and miracles of the Lie, and all the deception that sinfulness can impose on those doomed to destruction" (2 Thessalonians 2:4,6-10 NEB).

The *New Catholic Encyclopedia* (1966) states: "Catholic theologians have been nearly unanimous in maintaining that the anti-Christ will be an individual person. [The] anti-Christ is preserved, for the 'last times,' his tyranny to 'extend' to the second coming of Jesus Christ, who will vanquish and obliterate him, and set up His kingdom on earth."

Who is the Antichrist? As the *New Catholic Encyclopedia* points out, all through church history zealous prophets have audaciously identified certain characters or movements as "the Antichrist," only to fall thereby into theological discredit. The same source further indicates, as the apostle Paul clearly states, that while precursors of the Antichrist may well be harbingers of his coming (a point John made by saying these "many antichrists"), the real Antichrist will not be known until "someone or something," who [or which] restrains the forces of evil in general and the Antichrist in particular, is removed. This, of course, is based on the fact that Paul says clearly that the Antichrist will not be revealed until "the Restrainer disappears from the scene." Theologians throughout church history have been divided as to whether the Restrainer is the Church or the Holy Spirit. I would tend toward the latter view, but, either way, the meaning is not altered. On the Day of Pentecost, the Holy Spirit was given in a special way, as Jesus had repeatedly promised He would be, to call out and control the Church of Jesus Christ. And with the "gathering together unto Him (Christ)," the description of the rapture of the Church, the special gift of the Holy Spirit will be withdrawn.

Thus, with all true Christians in heaven with Christ —whether they be Calvinist or Armenian, Protestant or

Catholic, of the apostolic or charismatic age—on earth there will be no "Restrainer." Then, and then only, will be "the proper time" for the Antichrist to be revealed. From both scriptural and practical points of view it is as wrong to try to identify the Antichrist as it is to name a date for the return of Christ. Both errors have recurringly brought the preaching of biblical prophecy into needless and harmful disrepute, and this not only in the twentieth century, but all through church history.

What will be the empire of the Antichrist? Most encyclopedias, whether secular, Protestant, Catholic or secular; basing their view on Daniel 2 and 7 and Revelation 13 and 17, indicate generally that it will initially coincide with the ancient Roman Empire. (This view was given worldwide publicity through its expression in *The Omen*.) This empire will constitute a bloc of ten Western nations. When the Antichrist is on the ascendancy, according to the Apostle John, he will incorporate the power of ten rulers into his own iron grip "to share with the beast the exercise of royal authority; for they have but a single purpose among them and will confer their power and authority upon the beast" (Revelation 17:13 NEB).

With regard to chronological order, it seems that the war in which the Soviet military is largely destroyed as they try to descend into Israel will take place at the beginning of the "Great Tribulation." About then, the Antichrist will be killed, descend into perdition, and arise from the dead. Consolidating his hold in Jerusalem, he will send out his forces to conquer the world; he will rule with an iron hand, though his control will be short-lived. That the world is ominously awaiting such a dictator can be seen in the communiqué from the Club of Rome, which warns, "Crisis leads to war, and war today means nuclear conflagration, which in turns spells collective suicide . . . only a global plan . . . can avert universal catastrophe." Perhaps this case is put most convincingly by the Frenchman J. F. Revel in his *How Democracies Perish,* in which he reckons there's been "almost total Western intellectual" conversion to the one-world, strong-man concept.

When the Antichrist takes over, he will unify world currency, something which is well on its way to becoming a reality today with the advent of the cashless society with credit cards and electronic transfer of funds. On "The Today Show" (CBS,

January 29, 1985) "the Credit Card's Cousin, the Debit Card—a Plastic Check" was demonstrated as capable of completing the transition to a "cashless society" by 1990 if the full financial program were adopted. To make the system work would involve the capacity, through issuing numbers to people and placement of a "chip" (the "Mark of the Beast") on their hand or forehead, for a superman to gain total control over the masses. We read that the Antichrist (the Beast) "caused everyone, great and small, rich and poor, slave and free, to be branded with a mark on his right hand or forehead, and no one was allowed to buy or sell unless he bore this beast's mark, either name or number" (Revelation 13:16,17 NEB). Already the Netherlands is setting the precedent by issuing a number to every newborn baby. In the United States all workers must have a Social Security number; in Canada this is referred to as SIN (Social Insurance Number). Disney World in Florida offers an example of how an electronic scanner at a glance checks those who are "ticketed" in and out—to wit, an "invisible" mark on the hand.

But to accrue such monstrous magnetism as the Antichrist (as a worldwide dictator) will command, the question remains: Will moderns actually "worship the image of the Beast"? On "The Dick Cavett Show," Cavett alludes to a head of state he had on his program who "actually thought he was god!" UPI carries an article on the views of the British neurologist Dr. Frank Elliot, who had observed Joseph R. Stalin firsthand and had also studied Hitler. Elliot is of the opinion that many humans, once they're in power, are not only corrupted, but go mad and become megalomaniacs. They lose their capacity for emotion and can lie, steal, blame others, and become cruel and ruthless, losing the ability to feel guilt or shame. Therefore, to "worship the image of the Beast" is a credible potential for humanity. Secular humanists would have scorned this possibility until Hitler elicited a semblance of this kind of thing. Derek Taylor, the Beatles' press agent, observed the reaction they evoked when they were on tour. "It's absolutely rude, profane, vulgar; taken over the world, they are completely antichrist. Sick people rushed up. It was as if some saviour had arrived. The only thing left for the Beatles to do is to go on a healing tour. I'm antichrist, but these boys even shock me." Under the title "Growing Antichrist Movement in This Country," the *Minneapolis Tribune* argues that with Christianity effectively abolished from the schools, there is evidence everywhere that it now seems necessary "to infiltrate our schools with the occult, to the point of teaching it in classes": this, in my opinion, is just another step along the road to the coming world dictatorship.

In Matthew 24, Jesus intimates that when the Antichrist desecrates the Temple of God (as Daniel the prophet and St. John both indicate he will do with three-and-a-half years of his tenure left), he will bring such persecution upon believers that it will be a period which Jesus called the "great tribulation, . . . such as has not been from the beginning of the world." Forewarned Jesus, "So when you see 'the abomination of desolation,' of which the prophet Daniel spoke, standing in the holy place (let the reader understand), then those who are in Judaea must take to the hills. If a man is on the roof, he must not come down to fetch his goods from the house; if in the field, he must not turn back for his coat. Alas for women with child in those days, and for those who have children at the breast! Pray that it may not be winter when you have to make your escape, or Sabbath. It will be a time of great distress" (Matthew 24:15-21 NEB).

Looking for loopholes for unbelief and prodigal living, as man is always prone to do, many at this point ask: Is it not possible for me to reject Jesus Christ as Saviour and Lord here and now, and then be saved during that period of "great tribulation" to which Jesus referred, after the rapture of the Church to heaven? I do not believe so. For the Gospel preached during those terrible times will be to those who have never heard. Those who have heard and have rejected Christ as Savior and Lord will fall into the category of St. Paul's description in 2 Thessalonians 2:   The coming of the lawless one by the activity of Satan will be with all power and with pretended signs and wonders, and with all wicked deception for those who are to perish, because they refused to love the truth and so be saved. Therefore God sends upon them a strong delusion, to make them believe what is false, so that all may be condemned who did not believe the truth but had pleasure in unrighteousness (verses 9-11 RSV). Since this is the age of the Holy Spirit, the un-pardonable sin is being committed by those who ignore the

Spirit's call to Christ. When Jesus Christ comes to receive His Church and as we rise "to meet the Lord in the air," the present invitation of the Holy Spirit will be withdrawn.

When and where will the Battle of Armageddon be fought? The actual time is indicated by the prophet Daniel, by John in the Revelation, and by our Lord, as being just prior to the second coming of Jesus Christ to this earth. It will be, as I understand it, some time after Christ's coming to meet and receive His Church in the air, immediately prior to the revelation of Jesus Christ. It will be fought primarily on the plain of Megiddo (also referred to as Armageddon) the fourteen-by-twenty mile tract of land that Napoleon allegedly appraised as the most ideal place on earth for a military battle. It will also spill over into the Valley of Jehoshaphat (Joel 3) and southeast into Edom. Jerusalem itself will be the object of conquest for a bloodthirsty world.

"Armageddon," according to the *New Catholic Encyclopedia,* will be the place where the Antichrist will summon the kings of the earth for the final battle of mankind. The Northern, Southern, and Eastern blocs of nations will all converge to engage the Antichrist and his forces. The Russians will lead the Northern bloc, having only been partially destroyed earlier. The Southern bloc will be led by Egypt and will include both the Arab bloc of forty-one nations and the increasingly militant Organization of African Unity. Notes an Associated Press article (May 15, 1982), in "support of the Arab bloc in the Third World movement, there is near total isolation of Israel by black African countries." Egypt's increasing embrace of both blocs and sharpening antagonism toward Israel put them in a position of increasing likelihood to take such a position (*Toronto Star,* December 2, 1984). Sadat and much that he stood for is dead in Egypt today—as dead as the Pharaohs.

The fourth bloc of nations are the rulers of "the east." They are also referred to in Daniel 11 as converging in the Middle Eastern conflict, the centripetal nation of which is always Israel. In Revelation 9 and 16 these rulers are described as in command of an army of 200 million, these sweeping westward from beyond the Euphrates, which was the eastern boundary of the ancient Roman Empire. It appeared to be an astronomical figure to St. John, but China's chairman has widely publicized the fact that China now has a militia of 200 million, and proposes to use them to conquer the world. *Life's* John Saar is quoted in *Time* as getting the impression in Red China of a whole "population marshaled by a military system." "Let China sleep," Napoleon advocated, "for when China awakes let the nations tremble." And Japan—would they long lie low under the iron fist and heel of the Antichrist, with their capacity to mobilize their people and militarize their industries? And India and all Southeast Asia! They would doubtless smoulder in an irrepressible urge to rise up from under the oppression of the Antichrist.

The Antichrist will by now of course have excelled as a militarist—"in his estate shall he honor the God of forces" (Daniel 11:38). He'll have exercised such power as to have caused "fire to come down from heaven to earth [say, particle or laser beams, or nuclear power from a "Sky Wars" scenario in space] in full view of men" (Revelation 13:13 NIV). Television makes this possible, of course.

The War of Armageddon! Will it be the annihilation of all life on earth? No indeed! Rather it will usher out an old world and usher in a new one. Jesus likened it to "a woman when she is in travail hath sorrow, because her hour is come, but as soon as she is delivered of the child, she remembereth no more the anguish, for joy that a man is born into the world. [The world] shall have tribulation, but be of good cheer; I have overcome the world" (John 16:21,33; also see 1 Thessalonians 5:2,3). As the late Arnold Toynbee of Cambridge observed, "I believe the human race will not commit suicide—it will stop just short of that." Actually man would exterminate himself at Armageddon except for the fact that, just when it appears that he will destroy himself, Jesus, the real Christ, will come—and just in time.

The earliest prophecy known to be in print today is recorded in the epistle of Jude. It is a quote from "Enoch, the seventh from Adam," who foresaw this climax of history: "See, the Lord is coming with thousands upon thousands of his holy ones to judge everyone, and to convict all the ungodly of all the ungodly acts they have done in the ungodly way, and of all the harsh words ungodly sinners have spoken against him" (Jude 14,15 NIV). Jesus foresaw His second advent to earth and apprised His disciples who had gathered with Him on the Mount of Olives: "At that time they will see the Son of Man coming in a cloud with power and great glory" (Luke 21:27 NIV). For, as Zechariah predicted, the day of the Lord is coming, when He shall "gather all the nations against Jerusalem . . . on the east, and the Mount of Olives shall be split in two from east to west by a very wide valley; so that one half of the Mount shall withdraw northward and the other half southward" (Zechariah 14:2,4). This is something that seismologists have known for years is highly probable. In Revelation 16 it is called "a violent earthquake, like none before it in human history, so violent it was" (verse 18 NEB). In fact, as Dr. Charles Taylor points out, it will open up a waterway from the Mediterranean to the Dead Sea and drain southward through the Gulf of Aqaba into the Red Sea. Ezekiel prophesies of those millennial waters.

And so Jesus Christ the Lord will come on His white horse. At the time of President Reagan's inauguration in 1981, Johnny Carson asked, "Is President Reagan the Man on the White Horse, or the man in the White House?" President Reagan is the man in the White House. Jesus Christ is the Man on the White Horse yet to come. Paul wrote that Jesus will consume the Antichrist with the brightness of His coming. And that will be the moment when Israel as a nation will receive Jesus Christ as their Messiah. It will be, as Billy Graham said on national television (on December 8, 1984), the only time in history when a whole nation will, all at once, receive Jesus Christ as Saviour, Lord and King. As St. Paul wrote to the Romans (11:26), "All Israel shall be saved." Yes, a nation shall be born again in a day.

Both for magnificence and glorious truth, there is no more dramatic description in all literature than the following preview of the moment when our Lord returns to earth, as foreseen by John. In Revelation 19, he "saw heaven wide open, and there before me was a white horse; and its rider's name was Faithful and True, for he is just in judgment and just in war. His eyes flamed like fire, and on his head were many diadems. Written upon him was a name known to none but himself, and he was robed in a garment drenched in blood. He was called the Word of God, and the armies of heaven followed him . . . . [From] his mouth there went a sharp sword with which to smite the nations; for he it is who shall rule them with an iron rod, and tread the winepress of the wrath and retribution of God the sovereign Lord. And on his robe and on his leg there was written the name: King of kings, and Lord of lords" (Revelation 19:11-16 NEB). In the fourth century, the church father Jerome forecast, "No one shall be able to assist the antichrist as the Lord vents His fury upon him. Antichrist is going to perish in that spot from which our Lord ascended to heaven."

As the *New Catholic Encyclopedia* points out, the result of Christ's triumph over Antichrist and the forces of evil will be the advent of the millennium, a thousand-year reign of Jesus Christ and His saints of all the ages over an earth which will know unprecedented prosperity and peace. St. John foresaw in the Revelation, as Armageddon concludes with the glorious triumph of our Lord, how God bound Satan "for a thousand years . . . that he might seduce the nations no more till the thousand years were over." Furthermore, he "saw thrones, and upon them sat those to whom judgment was committed. I could see the souls of those who had been beheaded for the sake of God's word and their testimony to Jesus, those who had not worshipped the beast and its image or received its mark on forehead or hand. These came to life again and reigned with Christ for a thousand years, though the rest of the dead did not come to life until the thousand years were over. . . . They shall be priests of God and of Christ, and shall reign with Him for the thousand years" (Revelation 20:2-6 NEB).

"Everything we know," said Nobel Prize-winning chemist Willard Libby, "implies that the opportunities for future development are unbounded for a rational society operating without war." This, I suggest, will be realized during the earthly reign of our Lord.

From time immemorial, man has longed for a combination on this earth of law and order, peace and prosperity, freedom and fulfillment, health and happiness, godliness and longevity. It will happen when Christ comes again to this earth to set up His kingdom. The pope was right when he told the visiting rock group delegation, "It is not in my power to abolish war." Only Jesus Christ can do that. Two New York lawyers, Grenville Clark and Louis Sohn, wrote a classic entitled *World Peace Through World Law.* The question is: Who is to effect the "Law"? The answer is that peace and law can only happen when Christ comes again to install and implement them.

"In the last days," noted the ancient prophet Micah in a passage a United States president alludes to in his inauguration address, "it shall come to pass, that the mountain of the house of the Lord shall be established in the top of the mountains, and it shall be exalted above the hills; and people shall flow unto it. And many nations shall come and say, Come, and let us go up to the mountain of the Lord, and to the house of the God of Jacob; and he will teach us of his ways, and we will walk in his paths: for the law shall go forth of Zion, and the word of the Lord from Jerusalem. And he shall judge among many people, and rebuke strong nations . . . and they shall beat their swords into plowshares, and their spears into pruninghooks: nation shall not lift up sword against nation, neither shall they learn war any more" (Micah 4:1-4 KJV). Eric Sevareid, the CBS analyst, was so right to aspire for "the dawn of a new era [when] lions may lie down peacefully with lambs as the prophets foretold." *Time* tells us that while the number of the world's doctors, teachers, and engineers is currently increasing only slowly, the number of army officers is rising dramatically. The return of Christ will immediately reverse this. Indeed, there will be no need for the military at all, for Christ Himself will reign. Then and then only will be fulfilled the glorious vision of the ancient Isaiah, which no peace demonstration or human negotiations can effect: "The government shall be upon His [Jesus Christ's] shoulder and His Name shall be called Wonderful, Counsellor, the Mighty God, the Everlasting Father, the Prince of Peace. Of the increase of His government and peace, there shall be no end." And all the world will commune in symphony in literal fulfillment of our Lord's kingdom prayer:

> Our Father who art in heaven, Hallowed be Thy name.
> Thy Kingdom come, Thy will be done,
> On earth as it is in heaven.
> Give us this day our daily bread;
> And forgive us our debts. As we also have forgiven our
>   debtors;
> And lead us not into temptation, but deliver us from evil.
> For Thine is the kingdom and the power, and the glory, for
>   ever, Amen.

It was this that John Milton foresaw from the sixteenth century in *Paradise Restored,* as an answer to *Paradise Lost*: "At return of Him, thy Savior and Lord; in glory of the Father . . . [A] New earth, founded in righteousness, peace and love." Jonathan Edwards saw it in the Word of God in the eighteenth century, "As truly as I live, all the earth shall be filled with the glory of the Lord"; and across the Atlantic Isaac Watts was thinking not merely of Christmas, as we assume, but of Christ's future millennial reign over the earth when he lyricized:

> Joy to the world, the Lord is come.
> Let earth receive her King.
> Let every heart prepare Him room.
> And heaven and nature sing!
> He rules the earth with truth and grace.
> And makes the nations prove
> The glories of His righteousness,
> And wonders of His love!

And it was in the hallow of a climactic moment in the nineteenth century that Alfred, Lord Tennyson resounded:

> Ring out wild bells, to the wild sky.
> Ring out the old, ring in the new.
> Ring out the false, ring in the true.
> Ring out the feud of rich and poor.
> Ring out the want, the care, the sin.
> But ring the fuller minstrel in.
> Ring out the darkness of the land.
> Ring in the Christ that is to be.
> Ring out the thousand wars of old.
> Ring in the thousand years of peace.

Chapter Seven

Preparation for
His Coming

When I was at Oxford, I had the opportunity to hear C.S. Lewis who used to come back from Cambridge to give lectures. In one of his talks he said that a person may be about to be married, but, before the wedding takes place, Christ may come and call His responding bride to the marriage supper of the Lord. So, he said, make your first priority a preparation for that event. He went on: one may be a scientist on the verge of a society-changing invention, but, before he reaches his goal, Christ may come. So get ready now for that event. That way, instructed Lewis, you live in a constant state of meaningful expectation. Furthermore, every time the coming of the Lord is mentioned in the Scriptures, it is used as a basis for the Creator to say to His created, "Prepare to meet thy God."

More and more it appears to me that nearly everyone expects to have a showdown of some kind with God, somewhere, sometime. At the time of his death in 1983, Gordon Sinclair was the most outspoken agnostic in Canada. I was listening to his strong disapproval of the prima donna treatment a Toronto Maple Leaf hockey star was getting from the press. Sinclair stormed, "You'd think it was the second coming of Christ!" Calming down, he relented that he didn't know why he referred to the second coming of Christ, because he didn't believe in it. But many of his listeners, myself included, were not convinced.

Instinctively man has always somehow expected, whether in dread or welcome, an ultimate confrontation with God—a time when "every knee [shall] bow [and] every tongue [shall] confess that Jesus Christ is Lord, to the glory of God the Father." If he confesses here and now, it spells salvation forever with Christ. If he remains impenitent, it spells eventual submission, yes, but simultaneously a sentencing to the doom of the damned.

Two days before Jesus' trial and crucifixion, His disciples asked Him the fateful question. "What will be the signal for your coming and the end of this world?" Jesus' answer was a ninety-four-verse résumé of signs which, when fulfilled, would constitute the signal for His return to this earth to set up His kingdom. The whole treatise turns on verse 44 of Matthew 24: "Therefore be ye also ready: for in such an hour as ye think not, the Son of man cometh." Readiness: that's the key word; and it occurs several times in the New Testament with regard to the Lord's coming again.

Christ Himself is ready at any moment to return. As St. Peter puts it, He "stands ready to pass judgment on the living and the dead" (1 Peter 4:5 NEB). With His wondrous gift of eternal life, He is "already at the door!" (James 5:8,9, Phillips). Being the most festive event in history, the second coming is often compared in the Scriptures to a marriage, our Lord having gone to prepare a place for us and assuring us that "the wedding is ready"; or again, "All things are now ready."

Since believers are to expect the return of Christ at any moment, Jesus exhorted, "Your time is always ready." In short, we are to live in a state of perpetual readiness for His return. This was His message in the parable of the ten virgins: "They that were ready went." St. Paul begins his last chapter to Timothy with the "charge . . . before God, and the Lord Jesus Christ, who shall judge the quick and the dead at his appearing and his kingdom" (2 Timothy 4:1), and concludes: "Now the prize awaits me, the garland of righteousness which the Lord, the all-just Judge, will award me on that great Day; and it is not for me alone, but for all who have set their hearts on his coming appearance" (2 Timothy 4:8 NEB). Sandwiched between is the avowal: "I am ready."

Gwen Beck, a schoolteacher in Cody, Wyoming, where I

was holding a crusade, informed me that four years earlier her life had been constant confusion. A concerned sister on the East Coast sent her a copy of the first edition of my *Re-entry*. When Gwen read it, the warning of Jesus that we are to "be ready" for the coming again of Christ especially touched her. Gwen said, "I simply was not a Christian. This led me to confess on my knees that I was a sinner and I asked Christ to come into my life, and to be filled with the Holy Spirit." Jesus did just that, and with this new hope, Gwen's has been a life of unceasing fellowship and service to Christ.

The coming again of Jesus Christ is *imperative*. Man is so fast degenerating within and so inevitably being dashed headlong toward destruction from without that, apart from the intervention of God, he simply cannot save himself.

Lewis Thomas, in his 1984 best seller, *The Unforgettable Fire*, laments that his experiences both as a physician and a philosopher have assured him that in the late 1980s we earth-lings face "epidemic disease, meteorite collisions, volcanoes, atmospheric shifts in the levels of carbon dioxide, earthquakes, excessive warming or chilling of the earth's surface. [But we will not be] done in [by these]. We will do it to ourselves by warfare with thermonuclear weaponry, and it will happen." So reasons the secular-humanist.

Jesus foresaw this with divine precision when He replied to His disciples, who had inquired about the signs of His coming: "Then there will be great misery, such as has never happened from the beginning of the world until now, and will never happen again! Yes, if those days [were not] cut short, no human being would survive. But for the sake of God's people, those days are to be shortened" (Matthew 24:21,22, Phillips). So our Lord Jesus Christ will come again.

Out in front of our church, there was a sheet of ice, and my lovely wife and I were obliged to cross it to get to our car. Kathleen, who is from Ireland and not born with skates on her feet as Canadians have been thought to be, was gingerly looking down and cautiously picking every step. She thought that I was just ahead of her on her right; but someone had waylaid me, and I had dropped a few paces behind. Into the place I should have been strode a man with a clerical black coat like mine, also on his way to his car and walking charily. Reaching out and seizing his arm, my wife, without looking up, implored, "Darling, let me hang on to you or I will fall on this ice!" Overhearing her request I accelerated briskly, calling from behind, "Kathleen!" She thought at first that she was hearing stereo or something. Listening to our embarrassed apologies, the startled gentleman generously commiserated, "Anyone will latch on to anything on this slippery surface!"

Recuperating from the incident, it struck me: anyone will latch on to anything to keep from falling on the slippery surface which is the world today. And that is just what people are doing. Those who do not choose Christ and go to be with Him when He comes again are going to be reaching out in every direction as conditions in the world worsen. St. John in the Revelation of Jesus Christ foresaw this: "Then the kings of the earth, magnates and marshals, the rich and the powerful, and all men, slave or free, hid themselves in caves and mountain crags; and they called out to the mountains and the crags, 'Fall on us and hide us from the face of the One who sits on the throne and from the vengeance of the Lamb.' For the great day of their vengeance has come, and who will be able to stand?" (Revelation 6:15-17 NEB). Winston Churchill wept in the House of Commons as he reviewed "the awful unfolding scene of the future." In her syndicated column, Ellen Goodman asks of thinking people in the mid-1980s: With "Armageddon around the corner what are intelligent people to do? Wrap ourselves in mourning sheets and wait for the end? [We] are not talking about death, but extinction. Not talking about our future but about any future. This, while we see that nuclear sword of Damocles hung over us like some apocalypse without the promise of redemption." The last lament is what's wrong with the secularist.

Jesus urged us that when the apocalypse approached,"look up, and lift up your heads; for your redemption draweth nigh" (Luke 21:28). That's our hope: redemption! Only the Christian can stand up and be genuinely jubilant, for as St. Paul wrote to the Philippians, "Of one thing I am certain: the One who started the good work in you will bring it to completion by the Day of Christ Jesus" (Philippians 1:6 NEB).

St. Paul was certain of the Day of Christ because the coming again of the Lord Jesus is *immutable:* it is a changeless fact. Af-

firmed the writer to the Hebrews, "God, willing more abun-
dantly to shew unto the heirs of promise the immutability of his
counsel, confirmed it by an oath: that by two immutable things,
in which it was impossible for God to lie, we might have a
strong consolation"(Hebrews 6:17,18);"this is a powerful en-
couragement to us, who have claimed his protection by grasping
the hope set before us. That hope we hold. It is like an anchor
for our lives, an anchor safe and sure" (Hebrews 6:18,19 NEB).

I realize that some people find the facts of Christ's coming
again unbelievable. We have been told by NASA (*Toronto Star*
December 26, 1984) that by A.D. 2000 some people will have
moved to the moon where they'll live in air-conditioned
modules growing, among other things, tomatoes as large as
watermelons. They'll be surrounded by serving robots who'll
mine the moon as well as cook the food and make the beds. But
there's a problem. *Newsweek* reports that a poll was conducted
across America on who believed and who did not believe that
man had ever landed on the moon in the first place. Pollsters
were astounded at the percentage of people who believed that
the whole thing was a staged hoax. Why? Because the physics of
space travel were beyond them. They were not prepared to take
by faith what they couldn't understand. The fact that we can't
understand the astrophysics of Christ's coming again does not
alter the fact that He is coming.

Everybody wonders about the future, but no one knows exactly what the future holds. Alvin Toffler, author of *Future
Shock* and *The Third Wave,* comes out in 1985 with his
Previews and Premises, assuring us that without a transformation of our social institutions, man's future is more fragile than
at any time in human history. Actually, it's the spiritual
transformation of individuals by Jesus Christ that provides
hope for the future. Yet another Soviet leader takes over.
Surveying his task, he assesses: "The revolutionary transformation of society is impossible without changing man himself."
Exactly! But there is only One who can change many and,
through transformed people, transform society. It is Jesus
Christ! He does so by providing salvation for us in the present
and hope for the future. Believers in Christ know who holds the
future. And it is this confidence that the future is in Christ's
hands that gives us true hope in the present. St. Paul wrote to

the Romans, "Hope maketh not ashamed," and to Timothy he wrote, "I am not ashamed: for I know whom I have believed, and am persuaded that he is able to keep that which I have committed unto him against that day" (2 Timothy 1:12).

St. Paul was certain of one thing: the Day of Christ! Dean W. R. Matthews of St. Paul's Cathedral in London is right in saying that the world is living on a volcano, not a rock. But the Christian's hope rests, ultimately, not on military defenses but on the coming again of Christ. St. Paul wrote in 1 Corinthians 3:11, "Other foundation can no man lay, than that is laid, which is Jesus Christ." The superstructure the believer builds on this foundation will be manifest at the coming of Christ. The late Chief Justice Earl Warren claimed he always read the sports section first in his newspaper because it at least had some cheerful news; "The front page has nothing but man's failures," he wrote. In a world of gloom, man can turn to the Bible for the good news of Christ's coming again. A university student who was a star football player came forward in a crusade meeting one night to commit his life to Christ, explaining, "I got tired of playing the game without being able to see the goal posts." Without a goal, life has no direction.

A compass, wherever it is, always points north. So a believer's life should always point in the direction of Christ's coming again. "To me the second coming is the perpetual light on the path which makes the present bearable," reasoned G. Campbell Morgan. "I never lay my head on the pillow without thinking that perhaps before I awake, the final morning may have dawned. I never begin my work without thinking that He may interrupt it and begin His own." "Though He tarry past our time," reasoned Matthew Henry, "He will not tarry past the 'due time.' " There is a time, an exact time, on God's blueprinted schedule of events when Jesus Christ is due to return.

The coming again of Jesus Christ is *Immanuel,* that is, "God with us." Both in rapture and revelation, the return of our Lord will be personal. "If God is so wonderful," mused the little Italian girl, "why doesn't He show His face?" That is precisely what He *did* do in the person of Jesus Christ and *will* do again at Christ's second coming. "Behold he is coming," exulted John in Revelation 1 and "every eye shall see him, and among them those who pierced him; and all the peoples of the world shall lament in remorse. So it shall be. Amen. 'I am the Alpha and the Omega,' says the Lord God, who is and who was and who is to come" (Revelation 1:7,8 NEB). Perhaps John was thinking of that unforgettable moment when Jesus stood before the Sanhedrin in the house of Caiaphas, about to be condemned. Cross-examined by these green-eyed earthlings, our wonderful Lord burst forth in solitary assurance: that, one day, they would "see the Son of Man seated on the right hand of God and coming with the clouds of heaven" (Mark 14:62 NEB).

"The Lord himself shall descend," St. Paul assured the Thessalonians. On Ascension Day, on the Mount of Olives, the two white-draped figures who saluted the 500 upward-gazing disciples made the point that "this Jesus, who has been taken away from you up to heaven, will come in the same way as you have seen him go" (Acts 1:11 NEB). The theologian Bengel exegetes that the Greek present participle used here implies that the second advent, as the first, will be a bodily return of Jesus Christ.

A little girl from the farm was with her parents riding an elevator to the top of the high skyscraper. A Christian, she asked at the eighty-sixth floor, "Mommy, does Jesus know we're coming?" One thing among others is certain in the Bible, and that is that Jesus Christ knows we're going up to be with Him forever—because He is personally coming to get us. The historian Massilon wrote, "In the days of primitive Christianity, it would have been apostasy not to sigh for the return of the Lord." Every time the true Christian goes to the holy communion table to celebrate the Lord Supper, he must focus on the return of Christ to derive meaning, "This do in remembrance . . . till he come." Every time he goes to work, he ideally hears his Lord's words resound in his ears, "Occupy till I come" (Luke 19:13), for "blessed are those servants, whom the Lord when he cometh shall find watching" (Luke 12:37).

The coming again of Jesus Christ is *immense*: the most glorious "trip" man will ever have taken. St. Paul inspired the young preacher Titus with the ecstatic aspiration, "Looking for that blessed hope, and the glorious appearing of the great God and our Saviour Jesus Christ" (Titus 2:13). Just when it appears that the world is going up in smoke and man has reached his perigee, Jesus said, look to the apogee: "See the Son of Man coming on a cloud with great power and glory" (Luke 21:27 NEB). Orson Wells has described the perigee. With thermonuclear bombs "we can make a bonfire of all our works, empty our cities, scrape the living crust off our planet, and blast our habitation into a spinning globe of ash."

Queen Victoria left us a beautiful portrayal of the apogee. She was barely eighteen when she ascended the throne of the British Empire upon which the sun never set. Officially attending Handel's *The Messiah* for the first time, she was instructed: "The point at which the Hallelujah Chorus is sung, the entire audience will rise, as has been the custom since the days of George the First. But you are the Queen. You alone remain seated." When the glorious chorus was reached, all stood with military punctuality. Her Majesty alone remained seated. But when that thrilling, transcendent passage "King of Kings and Lord of Lords" was reached, the Queen rose and bowed, and not a member of the grand audience missed the significance.

Oh, what a day! "One day, Christ, the secret center of our lives, will show himself openly, and you will all share in that magnificent denouement," rejoiced St. Paul (Colossians 3:4, Phillips). St. Peter exulted, "When the Head Shepherd appears, you will receive for your own the unfading garland of glory" (1 Peter 5:4 NEB). "Eternal Glory to the Heroes" was *Izvestia's* prepared headline for the reentry of the *Soyuz II* trio. But glory was turned into gloom when the hatch door was opened and the cosmonauts were found strapped in their seats without any signs of life. This tragedy is in direct contrast to the coming of Christ, when death will be turned to life and gloom to glory.

As Chrysostom, that great preacher of the early, post-apostolic Church, was dying, he seemed to see the vision, "Glorious events; consummation events!" Called out Phil Jenks to his family, "Easy dying! Blessed dying! Glorious dying! I have experienced more happiness in two hours dying today than in my whole life!" S. B. Bangs put it, "The sun is setting; mine is rising. I go from this bed to a crown. Farewell!" Martha McCrackin rejoiced, "How bright the room, how full of angels!" Margaret Prior exulted, "The chariot has come and I am ready to step in." "Eternity rolls in before me like a sea of glory," exclaimed Jordan Ardie. "The One who can keep you from falling," pronounced St. Jude in his benediction, is the One who on the day of His coming will "set you in the presence of his glory, jubilant and above reproach" (Jude 24 NEB).

The second coming of Jesus Christ is indeed the perpetual light on the path of the believer, which makes the present delightful. If Jesus Christ is not coming again, we should close our Bibles and our churches. If we believe that He is indeed coming, the accusation of being cruel for remaining silent is not a strong enough indictment. We ought to study about His coming, sing about it, preach it, talk about it, write about it and spread the precious word of hope everywhere.

Said our Lord, "If anyone is ashamed of me and mine in this wicked and godless age, the Son of Man will be ashamed of him, when he comes in the glory of his Father and of the holy angels" (Mark 8:38 NEB). Eddie Fisher remarked on a radio program that during the course of the day he had discussed everything from ingrown toenails to the second coming of Jesus Christ. If ingrown toenails might be thought of as the low point of his conversation, certainly the high point was the second coming of Jesus Christ.

The coming again of Jesus Christ is *imminent*. No prophetic event or events await fulfillment prior to His coming for His Church. All of the New Testament writers exhort us to be "watching for," "waiting for," "looking for," "praying for," "hastening unto," and "expecting at any moment" the return of Christ. As Martin Luther said, "Christ deigned that the day of His coming should be hid from us, that being in suspense, we might be, as it were, on the watch." The signs to which reference has been made refer primarily to Christ's coming to this earth to set up His kingdom. But His "appearing" to His own in the air to withdraw His Church is referred to comparably often and always in the sense of its occurring at any moment. We are to be "looking for that blessed hope"; for to "them that look for him shall he appear": not at this time to all; just to ". . . them that look for him shall he appear" (Hebrews 9:28).

St. Paul wrote to the Thessalonians that "God hath not appointed us to wrath, but to obtain salvation" through His Son (1 Thessalonians 5:9). He defined Christians as those who "turned from idols, to be servants of the living and true God, and to wait expectantly for the appearance from heaven of his Son Jesus, whom he raised from the dead, Jesus our deliverer from the terrors of judgment to come" (1 Thessalonians 1:9,10 NEB). I feel sure that Paul was here referring to what would happen on earth to those who did not turn to Christ and so would be left to endure the consequent apocalyptic judgments. This same idea is to be found in the Revelation of Jesus Christ, where our Lord assures, "Because you have kept my command and stood fast, I will also keep you from the ordeal that is to fall upon the whole world and test its inhabitants. I am coming soon" (Revelation 3:10 NEB). To the Philippians, St. Paul admonished, "Let your magnanimity be manifest to all" for "the Lord is at hand." To the Corinthians, "You are not lacking in any spiritual gift" for the exercise of your testimony to Christ, as you are "waiting for the coming of our Lord Jesus Christ." So "be blameless in the day of our Lord Jesus Christ." To Timothy, Paul admonished, "Keep your commission clean and above reproach" for one day you will confront the "coming of Christ. This will be, in his own time, the final dénouement of God, who is the blessed controller of all things" (1 Timothy 6:13, Phillips).

Professor Duffield has pointed out that in the epistles alone there are twenty-two quotations calling us to purity, patience, and service in the light of Christ's return. The church father Cyril wrote 1,640 years ago, "Look thou for the Son of God to judge the quick and dead. Venture not to declare when, nor on the other hand slumber, for He saith, 'Watch.' We are looking for Christ." Adjudged the historian Gibbon, "As long as this error was permitted in the church, it was productive of most salutary effects on the practice of Christians." Dwight L. Moody, like Luther and Wesley, preached constantly that Christ's coming was imminent, declaring, "Nowhere am I told to watch for the millennium but for the coming of the Lord." Observed Howden, "Christ's coming is an event fraught with greater demands" than "were required at His first coming." Since Christ's coming is imminent, each of us must all times be at our best. A Soviet premier assures the world that "Communism is the wave of the future." The wave of our coming Lord is the expectation of every watching Christian, the wave of welcome which will greet the faithful with "Well done, good and faithful servant . . . enter into the joy of your Master" (Matthew 25:21 RSV).

The coming again of Jesus Christ is *immediate*. There will be no countdown for the coming down of our Lord to take us home. One Greek scholar calculates that the familiar "in the twinkling of an eye" of 1 Corinthians 15, which is read at nearly every Christian burial service, refers, as close as one can humanly conceive, to no time at all. That leaves no opportunity for the thief to repent or the prodigal to come home. Jesus did not say that His coming would be a clap of thunder, but "as the lightning." We can with some accuracy time thunder bursts by the lightning flash, because sound travels 186,000 miles per second. But lightning comes without a precursor.

Declared our Lord in His Revelation to John, "Behold, I come quickly, . . . hold fast to what you have—let no one deprive you of your crown. As for the victorious, I will make him a pillar in the Temple of my God." George Washington had a cook who was as prompt as the first U.S. president was truthful. "Gentlemen," said Washington to his guests, "I have a cook who never asks whether the company has come, but whether the hour has come!" "The hour is coming," said Jesus to His disciples, "when the dead will hear the voice of the Son of God, and those who hear will live." All of His disciples of that time fell into that category. Others, Jesus said later, will "tarry till I come." These could include you.

A United States senator reasons, "The hands of the clock are moving on toward midnight of the brief day left to us." "The clock of destiny," calculates Judge Wilkins, "tells the fateful hour." *Time* notes that "no one is able to see beyond the end of his nose. Profound bewilderment, foreboding, tragic uneasiness, fatalism," are only a few of the traits of our time. "Whom the gods would destroy," goes an ancient Greek proverb, "they first make mad." "If other planets are inhabited, they must be using this earth as a lunatic asylum," mused George Bernard Shaw. But I do not believe that a compassionate Jesus will permit the pressures of an age for which our minds were not designed to continue to build up until there is mass insanity. Instead He invites, "Repent for the kingdom of heaven is at hand."

Some years ago I received a letter from Paul Shields. He had been converted through the reading of my first edition of *Re-entry*. He wrote, "I was born the son of missionary parents while they were serving the Lord in Nigeria. While a teenager in Toronto, I rebelled. I began to smoke tobacco—then pot—to drink heavily, and after many violent confrontations with my parents I moved out. I became a drug addict, got married, had a kid, and moved to the West coast. My life turned from bad to worse. In Vancouver my drug addiction became chronic: soft drugs, hard drugs—and hard liquor. Finally, out of work, no money, heavily in debt, and my wife planning to separate from me, I was at the bottom. I knew it. I couldn't help myself at all. Disenchanted by my addiction, one Sunday night I remembered a book that had been put in my hand by some goody-two-shoes. It was *Re-entry*. I pulled it out and started to read. I couldn't put it down. The more I read, the more paralyzed with terror I became. Soon I fell under the conviction of the Holy Spirit. There I was alone at 3 A.M. crying my eyes out. I knew what I had to do. I had to give my heart to the Lord Jesus Christ, and ask Him to give me the peace and security I so desperately needed. I was instantly delivered, and have been ever since. My wife came to know the Lord. My life has been turned around." I first met Paul in Toronto at the Central Baptist Seminary, from which he graduated, later to be ordained into the ministry and serve as a Baptist pastor.

The coming again of Jesus Christ is *immigrational*. When does one become a citizen of the kingdom of heaven? When that person is born again! Wrote St. Paul to the Philippians, "We are citizens of heaven, and from heaven we expect our deliverer to come, the Lord Jesus Christ. He will transfigure the body belonging to our humble state, and give it a form like that of his own resplendent body, by the very power which enables him to make all things subject to himself" (Philippians 3:20,21 NEB). For this reason, as the apostle wrote to the Corinthians: "We never cease to be confident. We know that so long as we are at home in the body we are exiles from the Lord . . . we are confident, I repeat, and would rather leave our home in the body and go to live with the Lord" (2 Corinthians 5:6,8 NEB). Indeed, "we know that if the earthly frame that houses us today should be demolished, we possess a building which God has provided—a house not made by human hands, eternal, and in heaven. In this present body we do indeed groan; we yearn to have our heavenly habitation put on over this one—in the hope that, thus clothed, we shall not find ourselves naked. We groan indeed, we who are enclosed within this earthly frame; we are oppressed because we do not want to have the old body stripped off. Rather our desire is to have the new body put on over it, so that our mortal part may be absorbed into life immortal. God himself has shaped us for this very end; and as a pledge of it, he has given us the Spirit'' (2 Corinthians 5:1-4 NEB).

Ours is a world that groans, as St. Paul wrote to the Romans—groans for the redemption of the physical order, groans for freedom, groans for wholeness. Nina Simone, in what soul-singer Ray Charles calls "Message Things," is an international television sensation with her: "I wish I knew how it would feel to be free; I wish I could break all the chains holding me. I wish I could say all the things that I should say, Say 'em loud, say 'em clear, for the whole round world to hear." God's answer to this human yearning to be free and whole is to send back His Son.

David Lawrence expresses in *U.S. News and World Report,* "A climax of some kind seems to be approaching the world over." God's climax is the coming of Jesus Christ. Omar Bradley, the late American military general, observed incisively: "We know more about war than about peace, more about killing than about living. This is our twentieth century's claim to progress. Knowledge of science outstrips capacity for control. We have too many men of science; too few men of God. . . . The world has achieved brilliance without wisdom, power without conscience—a world of nuclear giants and ethical infants."

Will the world get ethically and spiritually better? Yes, but not until it gets worse, and Christ comes. "The facts," says *Intelligence Digest*, "show that the forces in the world struggle are grouping themselves for a decisive showdown." Man simply cannot better himself. Remarked that elder statesman Konrad Adenauer before his death, "Security and quiet have disappeared from the lives of men." The only answer is emigration to be with Christ for those who entrust themselves to Him. When the tyrannies of the Old World in Europe grew too great, the freedom lovers immigrated to a New World of freedom and challenge. Ruptured by a world of escalating pressures, one of these days Christians are going to be raptured to the glories of heaven.

What is eternally gratifying is that the coming again of Jesus Christ brings *immortality*. Jesus Christ came "to bring life and immortality to light through the gospel." When someone repents of sin and receives Christ as Savior and Lord, Jesus says, "I give them eternal life and they shall never perish" (John 10:28 NEB). Along comes Robert Ettinger, the father of cryogenics, to affirm: "There's no question that suspended animation will work. It's just a question of when." And so human beings are being frozen to wait a cure for the disease from which they died. But this of course is not an ultimate answer, since it will leave them mortal, subject again to death. Jesus Christ gives us "eternal life" with a body of immortality. "Lay hold on eternal life," exhorted St. Paul. Pop songs reveal how people yearn for a life and a relationship which will last. "Love Me a Million Years" sings one; and another, "Forever and a Day"; and another "From Here to Eternity." Arthur Clark, author of *2001: A Space Odyssey,* said to Walter Cronkite on CBS that he craves to live another twenty years and then he might be able to go on living forever. "The moon-walk goal is really a quest to live forever," observed that peerless science fiction writer Ray Bradbury on the same CBS program, adding, "This has been the quest of religion, politics, and science—to escape death."

We are living in a sad world. "If I were God," ruminated Goethe, "this world of sin and suffering would break my heart!" Jesus said to His disciples that, previous to His coming, there would be "the beginning of sorrows" which would then sharply increase. I saw the actual headline "The Beginning of Sorrows" in a paper recently. The World Health Organization says that in our world there are 11 million lepers; 50 million people with onchocerciasis; 190 million with filariasis; and 200 million with schistosomiasis.

We have already identified Jesus' forecast of famines as a harbinger of His return to earth. Annually, sixty-two million earthlings, deprived of food, wither away in famines and die from starvation. Who cares? Jesus does! And He's coming back surely and suddenly, sometime, to feed sumptuously and clothe lavishly those who otherwise would have perished in hunger. Meanwhile, the highest motivation for us to live selflessly is the anticipation of Jesus Christ's coming again. The president of the Lutheran Church in America noted the obscenity of *Time* having on one page pathetic, tragic pictures of starving people in Ethiopia, and alongside it an advertisement: "For the woman who has everything, think of gold this Christmas" (1984). In Pope John Paul II's Christmas homily, he picked up on St. John's ancient exhortation to the Laodiceans to prepare for Christ's coming again. The pope drew the contrast, "Are there not people rich in material goods, power, fame, and yet who are tragically poor? Poor by reason of the great emptiness of the human heart which has not opened itself to God. And are there not poor people who are materially disadvantaged, persecuted, oppressed, discriminated against who are rich? Rich with that inner wealth that flows directly from the heart of the God-Man Jesus Christ."

If there is a God, why doesn't He show? snaps the agnostic. He has already: 2,000 years ago in His incarnation. And He will show again. Jesus Christ is coming and, as His Revelation previews, "Behold, the tabernacle of God is with men, and he will dwell with them, and they shall be his people, and God himself shall be with them, and be their God" (Revelation 21:3). And God shall "wipe every tear from their eyes; there shall be an end to death, and to mourning and crying and pain; for the old order has passed away" (Revelation 21:4 NEB). Only immortality with Christ can provide such a wonderful life. "At the moment, efforts to lengthen the life span seem to have broken down," states the *New York Times*. It goes on to indicate: "The conquest of cancer, heart disease and the like will not lead to a dramatic increase in the life span. Too many weaknesses are built into the human frame to be overcome." What is the answer? A new body in which mortality gives way to immortality. The man was right who said, "Those who take no care for the future, soon sorrow for the present."

The coming again of Jesus Christ is *implicational*. "Yes, I am coming soon," stressed our Lord in the final chapter of the Bible, "and bringing my recompense with me, to requite everyone according to his deeds!" (Revelation 22:12 NEB). Throughout the New Testament, it is clearly taught that when

Christ appears for His Church, the first item on the agenda will be the review of believers' works. Thereupon prizes, crowns and rewards will be distributed and status in the life hereafter conferred according to our faithfulness. "For we must all have our lives laid open before the tribunal of Christ," St. Paul apprised the Corinthians, "where each must receive what is due to him for his conduct in the body, good or bad" (2 Corinthians 5:10 NEB). On this basis, he admonished: "Pass no premature judgment; wait until the Lord comes. For he will bring to light what darkness hides, and disclose men's inward motives; then will be the time for each to receive from God such prizes as he deserves" (1 Corinthians 4:5 NEB).

It is understandable then that St. Paul should bring to a climax that chapter devoted to the coming again of Christ, 1 Corinthians 15, with, "Therefore, my beloved brothers, stand firm and immovable, and work for the Lord always, work without limit, since you know that in the Lord your labour cannot be lost" (1 Corinthians 15:58 NEB). Similarly, 1 Thessalonians, which St. Paul devoted to the denouement events, is brought to a climax with the aspiration, "May the God of peace make you holy through and through. May you be kept in soul and mind and body in spotless integrity until the coming of our Lord Jesus Christ" (1 Thessalonians 5:23, Phillips). St. Peter shared the same ultimate concern: "In view of the fact that all of these things are to be dissolved, what sort of people ought you to be? Surely men of good and holy character, who live expecting and earnestly longing for the coming of the day of God" (2 Peter 3:11,12, Phillips). Added the aged St. John: "Yes, now, little children, remember to live continually in him. So that if he were suddenly to reveal himself we should still know exactly where we stand, and should not have to shrink away from his presence" (1 John 2:28; Phillips). Going on to give a vivid account of the coming again of Christ, St. John sums up, "Everyone who has at heart a hope like that keeps himself pure, for he knows how pure Christ is" (1 John 3:3, Phillips).

A very vigorous controversy in American government for many years has been how much of the G.N.P. should be spent on exploration of space. Currently the estimate is one percent. Frank Borman, currently president of Eastern Airlines, is a potent protagonist of the concept that an escalated emphasis on space exploration will assist rather than diminish the solution of the problems of poverty and pollution here on earth. For example, the *Discovery* and *Challenger* spaceships were able to monitor the movement of the Sahara southward into the central Africa greenbelt which thereby escalated famine in places like Niger and Chad; solutions could then be prescribed. They were also able to spot mineral distribution and wealth deep in the earth by the highly sophisticated equipment aboard. If man could invent equipment to discover treasure on (and under) the earth from the heavens, how much more can Jesus' exhortation to lay up treasures in heaven be realized by faithful believers on earth!

Asked what the greatest thought that ever crossed his mind was, Daniel Webster replied, "My accountability to Almighty God." "There is no such incentive to evangelism," reckoned D. L. Moody, "as the pre-millennial coming of our Lord. Emphasize what God hath emphasized." In the Presbyterian Confession of 1967, it is pointed out that "the life, death, resurrection and promised coming of Jesus Christ have set the pattern for Church mission." Think of what a congregation like the Peoples Church of Toronto does to evangelize the world. In addition to the hundreds of workers who have gone forth from the congregation through the years, a million and a half dollars are being given annually for foreign missions to get the Gospel out to the ends of the earth. What rewards will be forthcoming at Christ's return to those who pray, give, or go forth to evangelize the world! Christ is coming. What an incentive to evangelize!

Finally, the coming again of Jesus Christ is *impending*. Whether the Scriptures are referring to the appearance of Christ for His Church or His coming to earth to set up His kingdom, reference to His return always has attached to it the urgent exhortation to be ready. Oh, the drama and import of Jesus' words! "So shall it be in that day when the Son of man is revealed. . . . Two women shall be grinding together; the one shall be taken, and the other left. Two men shall be in the field; the one shall be taken, and the other left" (Luke 17:34-36). "Watch ye therefore," warned our Lord, "for ye know not when the master of the house cometh, at even, or at midnight, or at the cockcrowing, or in the morning: lest coming suddenly he find

you sleeping. And what I say unto you I say unto all, Watch''
(Mark 13:35-37).

Christian, never let the realization fully escape your consciousness that at any moment Christ may come again. Be
always, and do always, those things which would please your
Lord were He to come this minute. In Joel's ancient prophecy
we read, "Multitudes, multitudes in the valley of decision. The
day of the Lord is near in the valley of decision." In the light of
the Lord's coming, Joel gave us that Gospel promise which has
been quoted wherever heralds of salvation have gone. "And it
shall come to pass, that whosoever shall call upon the name of
the Lord shall be delivered" (Joel 2:32). To be rightly related to
Jesus Christ is to be ready for His coming again. As Neil Armstrong stepped on to the moon, he declared, "One small step for
man; one giant leap for mankind!" The Chinese have an old
proverb: "The journey of a thousand miles begins with the first
step." Certainly the journey to heaven begins with one step: the
step of faith which puts our foot down on the promise of the
Word of Christ that He will take to His celestial and eternal
home all who on this earth place their firm belief in Him as
Savior and Lord. Only that person can join in the final aspiration of Scripture, "Even so, come, Lord Jesus!"

There is one teaching that is more important than the
preaching of the second coming of Christ. It is the preaching of
the Christ of the second coming. The two are inseparable, of
course. From ancient times, the proclamation of the former has
turned millions of people to seek the latter. St. Paul wrote to the
Corinthians in his first epistle, at the end of the fifteenth
chapter, that magnificent account of the second coming of
Jesus Christ! But the magnificence of that passage is matched
by the first four verses which express in essence and comprehen-
sion the clear plan of salvation, "Moreover, Brethren, I declare
unto you the gospel, which I preached unto you, which also ye
have received and wherein ye stand; by which also ye are saved,
if ye keep in memory what I preached unto you, unless ye have
believed in vain. For I delivered unto you first of all that which I
also received, how that Christ died for our sins according to the
scriptures; and that he was buried, and that he rose again the
third day according to the scriptures." That, my friend, is the
Good News, the Gospel, God's plan for you to be forever

saved, to be ready to go when Christ comes again.

On September 5, 1953, during a month-long crusade in Britain, I preached a message on the second coming of Christ. I was recently informed that in the packed crowd in the large tent that night was Constable Baird, his gracious wife, and his three sons—Trevor, aged nineteen; Neville, fourteen; and Clifford, eight. At the end of the address and in response to the invitation of Jesus to do so, many people came forward and gave their lives to Christ. Among those confessing Christ were Constable and Mrs. Baird and a very decisive and determined Clifford. He was forever changed. On the way home that night, the father asked Neville and Trevor, "Should the Lord come again tonight, would you go to be with Him?" They didn't think they would. After a grave spiritual struggle, fourteen-year-old Neville made his response on September 22, and about a week later, Trevor did so. They were completely changed by giving their lives to Christ. Today Clifford is a psychologist and university instructor living a life of enthusiastic service for Christ, as is his brother Neville and their families in Wheaton, Illinois.

Trevor served for a dozen years as minister of one of Canada's great churches, where it was my privilege to preach. He asked me to speak there on the second coming of Christ, which I did. That night his son Stephen, aged nineteen, came forward to surrender his life to Jesus. Trevor exclaimed, "That's three generations of my family—my parents, the three of us brothers, and now my son—all coming to the Lord through your preaching the message of the second coming of Christ."

Friend, before you put this book down, ask yourself, "Am I a total believer in the Lord Jesus Christ as my personal Savior and Lord? If Jesus were to come this moment, is my life entirely His?" If you have the slightest doubt, pray this prayer to Christ, who actually is on the doorstep of your life, "Lord Jesus Christ, come into my life in all your fullness, cleanse me by your shed blood from all of my sins, and fill me with your Holy Spirit. Help me to read your Word each day. And help me always to be ready for your coming again by daily prayer and the determination to share my faith with others in the worship and fellowship of your church. I thank you, Lord Jesus Christ."

If you have made that your prayer, and you'd like counseling materials to further your faith in Christ and fellowship in His Church, write to me today:

Dr. John Wesley White
Box 100
Milliken, Ontario L0H 1K0
Canada